The 9/11 Handbook

edited by

Hans G. Kippenberg

and

Tilman Seidensticker

The 9/11 Handbook

Annotated Translation and Interpretation of the Attackers' *Spiritual Manual*

edited by

Hans G. Kippenberg

and

Tilman Seidensticker

Equinox Publishing Ltd

equinox

London Oakville

Published by

UK: Equinox Publishing Ltd., Unit 6, The Village, 101 Amies St., London SW11 2JW
USA: DBBC, 28 Main Street, Oakville, CT 06779

www.equinoxpub.com

First published 2006

Library of Congress Cataloguing-in-Publication Data
The 9/11 handbook : annotated translation and interpretation of the attackers' Spiritual Manual / edited by Hans G. Kippenberg and Tilman Seidensticker.
p. cm.
Includes bibliographical references and index.
ISBN 978-1-84553-129-4 (pb)
ISBN 1-84553-129-9 (pb)
1. September 11 Terrorist Attacks, 2001. 2. Terrorism--Religious aspects--Islam. 3. Qaida (Organization) I. Kippenberg, Hans G. (Hans Gerhard) II. Seidensticker, Tilman. III. Title: Nine-eleven handbook.
HV6432.7.A1285 2006
973.931--dc22

2006023680

Typeset by Forthcoming Publications Ltd.
www.forthcomingpublications.com

Printed and bound in Great Britain by Lightning Source UK Ltd., Milton Keynes and Lightning Source Inc., La Vergne, TN

Contents

Preface

Subsequent to the 2003 annual meeting of the *Deutsche Vereinigung für Religionsgeschichte* (German Association for the History of Religion), dedicated to 'Religion and Conflict', the *Spiritual Manual* of the 9/11 attackers became the subject of a round table talk, held at the Max-Weber-Kolleg of the University of Erfurt. The document was presented in a German translation, and some crucial aspects were treated in academic papers. That round table event was the nucleus of a book published in 2004 in German: *Terror im Dienste Gottes. Die 'Geistliche Anleitung' der Attentäter des 11. September 2001* (Frankfurt/New York). Since then several studies have appeared, adding substantially to our understanding of the events of 9/11. While in 2003 suspicions of a forgery circulated, these doubts faded after serious research. The document turned out to be the handbook by which the attackers actually prepared their crime and conceived of it as a sacred deed. In contrast to the rising scholarly consensus, the official *9/11 Commission Report*, published by the US government and Congress in 2004, ignored the document completely.

In light of these shifting understandings of the subject, the editors of this book decided that an English publication should not confine itself to a translation of the earlier German book. The Arabic text, published on the website of the FBI, was checked again, the edition amended in about a dozen places, a fresh translation made, mistakes in previous publications eliminated, and commentaries added to the translation. The focus of the English edition has been changed slightly; as such, two chapters of the German original have been omitted, while a new chapter (Chapter 8) has been written especially for this new version. Our wish is to present a reliable and concise account for all who want to know more about the background to the events of 9/11: for journalists, politicians, students, and teachers from various academic disciplines.

The authors wish to express their thanks to Suzanne Eggins for her careful editorial work, and to Patrick Wöhrle for compiling the index. Tilman Seidensticker thanks Peter Seidensticker, Isabel Huck, and, above all, Kathrin 'Tini' Enke for their help in finding an appropriate English expression for difficult matters. Hans G. Kippenberg acknowledges gratefully the assistance of Karola Kippenberg in preparing a first English translation of his contributions.

Hans G. Kippenberg
Max-Weber-Kolleg, University of Erfurt

Tilman Seidensticker
Friedrich Schiller University of Jena

1

BACKGROUND TO THE *SPIRITUAL MANUAL*: ITS DISCOVERY, INTERROGATION, AND DISREGARD

Hans G. Kippenberg

At a Press conference on 28 September 2001, the FBI distributed four pages of an Arabic document, and also published it on its website, where it can still be found today (see Fig. 1, next page).[1] The headline is spectacular: 'Hijacking letter Found at three Locations'. Beneath the four pages of Arabic text spread out across the webpage, the FBI displays three photos, accompanied by information about the hijackers, their flights, and the places where the documents were found. The photo of Mohammed Atta links him with American Airlines flight 11 which crashed into the North Tower of the World Trade Center at 8:45. Underneath Atta's photo is the statement: 'Found in Atta's suitcase'. The next photo shows Nawaf al-Hazmi. The commentary connects him with American Airlines flight 77, which crashed into the Pentagon at 9:39. A line beneath his photo states that the document was 'Found in Vehicle at Dulles International Airport', Washington. Finally, a photo of the crash site of United Airlines flight 93 at Stony Creek Township is accompanied by the remark: 'Found at Crime Scene'.

1. *Provenance of the Document*

Mohammed Atta, who navigated the first plane into the North Tower of the World Trade Center, began his journey in Portland and changed planes in Boston. One piece of his luggage did not make it into his plane from Logan Airport Boston to Los Angeles: a security screening system in Portland withheld his bag from the plane to Boston.[2] When it was found later, two documents were discovered inside it. In a last will, made

Figure 1. *The website of the FBI (28 September 2001) displays four pages of the Arabic text, along with information about the locations where they were found: in Mohammed Atta's suitcase, in the vehicle of Nawaf al-Hazmi at the airport of Washington and at Stony Creek Township where one of the planes crashed.*

in 1996, Atta prescribed how his body should be handled after his death in order to prevent ritual pollution.[3] When he signed his will, he did not expect to die as a martyr, since the body of a martyr is buried without ritual washing. Apparently his last written will has nothing to do with his premeditated death five years later.

More dramatic is a handwritten Arabic text that was published by the FBI. It was written on four sheets, listed by the FBI as K 70 0109 17003 HC. The text anticipates three stages of the attack and for each stage prescribes recitations of the Koran, prayers and rituals. On 30 September 2001, the British newspaper *The Observer* published an English translation of the four pages.[4] An improved translation was later made by Hassan Mneimneh for *The New York Review of Books*;[5] recently David Cook has published another translation.[6]

The text found in Mohammed Atta's bag was not the only copy. A second copy was found in the car left by Nawaf al-Hazmi at Dulles International Airport, Washington. CBS News claimed to have obtained that copy, and on 1 October 2001 published an English translation.[7] This text was written on two sheets only, using the front and back of the pages. The two sheets were registered with the FBI as 0109 18019 K 655. The CBS translation accords completely with translations of Mohammed Atta's text. Since all scans available on the Internet reproduce one and the same text, the four sheets belonging to Mohammed Atta are presumably a photocopy of the text associated with Nawaf al-Hazmi. Remnants of the third copy have not been published.

On 28 September 2001, *The Washington Post* published a leading article on the discovery, headlined 'In Hijacker's Bags, a Call to Planning, Prayer and Death'. The article mentioned five sheets instead of four, and later in the same issue (page A18) two extracts in English were published:

> In the name of God, the most merciful, the most compassionate.... In the name of God, of myself and of my family...I pray to you God to forgive me from all my sins, to allow me to glorify you in every possible way.
>
> Remember the battle of the prophet...against the infidels, as he went on building the Islamic state.

Since neither extract can be traced to the four pages, it is reasonable to assume that they derive from the alleged fifth page. The second quotation accords perfectly with the *Spiritual Manual* (as we shall refer to the text from now on), since it conceives of the attacks in terms of the Prophet Muḥammad's military actions—after leaving Mecca for Medina, Muḥammad began establishing an Islamic polity by force. But the first extract immediately elicited doubts about its authenticity. What pious Muslim would dare to say: 'In the name of God, of myself and of my family'? Since the FBI has not released the Arabic original of this text, a mistranslation cannot be ruled out.

The document and all information about it derive from US Secret Service sources—a fact that has given rise to speculations of a forgery. It is important to note, therefore, that some independent evidence about the *Spiritual Manual* exists. It derives from a reporter for al-Jazeera, the Qater-based Arabic TV station, Yosri Fouda, who under conspiratorial circumstances met Ramzi Binalshibh in 2002 in Karachi. Binalshibh, from Yemen, was the intermediary between the Hamburg group and the chief of the military committee of al-Qaeda, Khalid Sheikh Mohammed. In an extensive interview Binalshibh told Yosri Fouda how the attacks were prepared, and during the interview showed him a suitcase with 'souvenirs' from his stay in Hamburg, among them a booklet on flight manoeuvres:

> 'Wait, wait', Fouda said as Ramzi tried to line up even more souvenirs. Next to a series of sophisticated illustrations on 'How to perform sudden manoeuvres', Fouda's eye had caught a page with paragraphs underlined and appended with handwritten notes. 'It is brother Abu 'Abdu'l Rahman's handwriting', said Ramzi, referring to Atta by his al-Qaeda kunyah. It did not look much like the rather prettier handwriting in the chilling 'Manual for a Raid' document that had been found in the luggage Atta had left behind at Logan Airport and which up to this point had always been attributed to him... Ramzi explained the discrepancy in the handwriting. Atta was not the author of the instructions and prayers found in the luggage. They had been written by Abdulaziz al-Omari, Atta's fellow hijacker and companion during the last hours of his life. Al-Omari, although one of the youngest of the hijackers, was recognized by the rest as having an exceptional knowledge of Islam—and a neat hand. This discovery confirmed what Mohammed Atta senior had been saying since the emergence of this document. 'My son's is a funny handwriting', he said, '...you could not tell if it belonged to a small kid or to a city planner'.[8]

According to Ramzi Binalshib, the author of the *Manual for a Raid*, as the document became known, or the *Spiritual Manual* as we refer to it in this book, was Abdulaziz al-Omari. Binalshibh's information is not implausible, since the composer of the *Spiritual Manual* was highly engaged in Islam, but was certainly not an educated Islamic cleric. This is in agreement with the instructions for the last night:

> Know that the best way of recitation is reciting the Noble Koran according to a consensus of the scholars *as far as I know.*[9]

The words 'as far as I know' indicate a lay person as author. Similar phrases recur in 3/1 and 3/14. In Islam, clerics are legal experts, while sermons are often delivered by lay persons.

Regarding al-Omari, the *9/11 Commission Report* supplied some additional information:

> Omari had graduated with honors from high school, had attained a degree from the Imam Muhammad Ibn Saud Islamic University, was married and had a daughter. He 'often served as an imam at his mosque in Saudi Arabia'. Omari 'is believed to have been a student of a radical Saudi cleric named Sulayman al-Alwan. His mosque, which is located in al Qassim Province, is known among more moderate clerics as a 'terrorist factory'.[10]

Shortly after the interview, Ramzi Binalshibh was arrested, and vanished into an American prison. Since the tapes of the interview were still in his possession because he wanted to sell them to al-Jazeera, Yosri Fouda's report cannot be checked. All in all, however, it appears reliable.

2. *Suspicions of a Forgery*

From the very beginning, the authenticity of the document elicited doubts. Immediately after its release, the well-known Middle East scholar Robert Fisk drew attention to sentences in the document that he found suspicious 'What Muslim would write: 'The time of fun and waste is gone'?' he asked in *The Independent* on 29 September 2001.[11] Fisk's remarks gained additional weight in conjunction with various conspiracy theories that started circulating soon after the events. Michael Barkun, who had studied the American culture of conspiracy for many years, had no difficulty linking certain stories about the attack and the reaction of the US government to long established types of conspiracy. Some American groups did not attribute the attacks to Usama bin Ladin and his organization, but to an attempt by the US government to restrict the freedom of its citizens under the pretext of counterterrorism.[12] Other conspiracy theories originated outside the United States. Rumors swept across the Muslim world that the attacks were perpetrated by the Israeli Secret Service and that four thousand Jews who normally worked in the World Trade Center did not show up for work on 11 September, because they had been tipped off by Mossad.[13] In fact, Israelis died in the attacks.[14]

Not all Muslims regarded the attack as a Jewish conspiracy. On various occasions following 9/11, Usama bin Ladin privately expressed his support for the attack, and in 2004 he publicly admitted his involvement in its planning.[15] In addition, some of the perpetrators left farewell videos testifying to their intention to attack the United States and to die as martyrs. A message by Ahmad Ibrahaim al-Haznawi al-Ghamidi from Saudi-Arabia, a member of the team heading for Washington, DC, was broadcast by al-Jazeera on 15 April 2002. Al-Haznawi declared that 'we left our families' in order to send a message: that it is time to kill the Americans in their own backyard and to ask God for martyrdom: 'O God, I sacrifice myself for your sake, accept me as martyr'.[16] In April 2002, a communiqué from al-Qaeda proudly mentioned the recorded testaments of the attackers and cited Islamic traditions in support of the operations in New York and Washington.[17] In September 2002, al-Jazeera broadcast a farewell video by Abdulaziz al-Omari:

> I am writing this with my full conscience and I am writing this in expectation of the end, which is near… God praise everybody who trained and helped me, namely the leader Sheikh Usama bin Ladin.

Al-Jazeera also showed footage of Ahmed al-Nami, Hamza al-Ghamdi, Said al-Ghamdi, and Walid al-Shehri in Kandahar, Afghanistan, studying maps and flight manuals. Given this evidence, it is improbable that anybody other than the Muslim fighters carried out the attack.

Even so, a forgery of the *document* by the FBI remains possible, though highly improbable. Forgery is a common phenomenon in the history of religions. Well-known documents are ascribed to authorities who could not have written them. For example, neither the biblical fifth book of Moses nor the book of Daniel were composed by the authors or in the time they pretend, but by others and much later. In these and other instances the suspicion of forgery has been substantiated by scholarly inquiry, where careful investigation and discussion has eventually established the suspicion as a plausible thesis. In the case of our document, however, it is quite the other way around. The advocates of a forgery did not make any serious attempts to prove their claim. They did not address such crucial issues as: Who was responsible for the forgery? What was the purpose of it? Who used the forged document and for what aim? Since these questions are not even raised, the notion of a forgery is without any scholarly value and must be seen as part of a conspiracy theory.

3. *Denying 'Terrorists' a Religious Faith*

Surprisingly, the *Spiritual Manual* nearly disappeared completely from public debates in the United States.[18] Nothing illustrates this better than the *Final Report of the National Commission on Terrorists Attacks upon the United States*. The Commission had been installed by Congress and the President in November 2002 and submitted its findings in 2004 as

The 9/11 Commission Report.[19] The report reconstructs with scrupulous detail the chain of events leading to the attack but completely ignores our document. The *Spiritual Manual* required all fighters to perform rituals, recitations, and prayers throughout the night before the attacks. According to the *Commission Report*, however, Mohammed Atta and Abdulaziz al-Omari that night pursued 'ordinary activities: making ATM withdrawals, eating pizza, and shopping at a convenience store'.[20] The emphasis on 'ordinary activities' can be read as a deliberate denial of a religious preparation of the act. An additional *Staff Report of the Commission*, outlining the details of the 9/11 plot, likewise ignored the existence of the document. We are told about the luggage of Mohammed Atta (and Abdulaziz al-Omari), in which the document was found:

> The luggage they checked in Portland failed to make it onto the plane. Seized after the September 11 crashes, Atta and Omari's luggage turned out to contain a number of telling items, including: correspondence from the university Atta attended in Egypt; Omari's international driver's license and passport; a video cassette for a Boeing 757 flight simulator; and this [*sic*] folding knife and pepper spray, presumably extra weapons the two conspirators decided they didn't need.[21]

This disregard for the document is reinforced by the manner in which the *Commission Report* conceived of the perpetrators.

> We learned about an enemy who is sophisticated, patient, disciplined, and lethal. The enemy rallies broad support in the Arab and Muslim world by demanding redress of political grievances, but its hostility toward us and our values is limitless. Its purpose is to rid the world of religious and political pluralism, the plebiscite, and equal rights for women. It makes no distinction between military and civilian targets. *Collateral damage* is not in its lexicon.[22]

According to the *Commission Report*, the perpetrators are inspired by a hatred for humanity, not by a dedication to their own cause or their own faith. In contrast to this assumption, the *Spiritual Manual* shows a different category of perpetrator: a person committing a crime out of a conviction. The US definition of a terrorist seems to have inspired the portrayal of the attackers as manifestations of an evil, performing atrocities for their own sake. In 1983, the US State Department had defined terrorism as follows:

> The term 'terrorism' means premeditated, politically motivated violence perpetrated against non-combatant*[23] targets by subnational groups or clandestine agents, usually intended to influence an audience.

This definition avoids any comment on the legitimacy of resistance against foreign occupation. According to a protocol added to the Geneva Convention on 8 June 1977, the international rules for conducting war were expanded to include freedom fighters, while at the same time, the rules rejected violence against civilians in this kind of war. In defiance of that rule, the US definition suspended the dialectics of 'One Person's Terrorist is Another's Freedom Fighter'.[24] Instead, it split the notion into two opposing categories: genuine freedom fighters, supported by the United States; and inhuman terrorist organizations, listed annually by the US State Department and persecuted globally. While in reality people—and in particular freedom fighters—are ethically both bad and good at the same time, the definition splits that reality into two camps: the adherents of civilization and the manifestations of evil.

Tomis Kapitan, an American philosopher focusing on issues of international ethics, has scrutinized the effects the split had upon the rhetoric of the notion 'terrorists'. Kapitan points out that it erases any incentive to understand the terrorists' point of view; it deflects attention away from policies that may have contributed to their grievances; it repudiates any calls to negotiate with them; and it implies that force and violence are the only adequate and proper means of dealing with them. Terrorists are beyond the international legal order.[25] When President Bush declared the war on terror, he signed an internal memo concerning the 'Humane Treatment of al Qaeda and Taliban Detainees' on 7 February 2002. As Commander-in-Chief he determined that none of the provisions of the Geneva Convention apply to the conflict with al-Qaeda. The values of the American nation require the Armed Forces to treat al-Qaeda captives humanely, but only insofar as this treatment is 'appropriate and consistent with the military necessity'. This restriction paved the way for the illegal practices at the Abu Ghraib and Guantanamo detention centres.[26]

Despite all doubts and uncertainties, attempts have been made to take the *Spiritual Manual* seriously. In January 2002, Hassan Mneimneh and Kanan Makiya published an examination of the *Manual for a 'Raid'*, followed by a translation in *The New York Review of Books*, as mentioned above. The authors checked the content of the document with regard to Islamic literature, theology, and history. In the end they did not conclude that it was a forgery, but something they regarded as a serious distortion of Muslim traditions: a deeply subversive form of political and ideological militancy.[27] In December 2002, the Martin-Marty-Center of the University of Chicago, a research institution for the study of religions, started a debate about the document on its website.[28] Bruce Lincoln, following up on the points made by Mneimneh and Makiya, specified the worldview of the perpetrators by pointing to the Egyptian intellectual Sayyid Quṭb, a spokesman of militants among the Muslim Brotherhood in the 1960s. Sayyid Quṭb denounced the Westernization of Egypt's culture and society as a new paganism, a new era of ignorance (*jāhiliyya*). He called upon the faithful Muslim to do the same as the prophet had once done: to violently overthrow the power of paganism, acting together with a few dedicated men. Sayyid Quṭb paid for his subversive version of Islam with his life and was executed by the Egyptian government in 1966.[29] Bruce Lawrence and Mark Juergensmeyer joined the debate on the Chicago website and supported Lincoln's assessment. Good reasons exist, therefore, to be less afraid of a forgery than of missing a unique chance to reconstruct the meaning the attackers attributed to their deed.

It took three years after the document was found before the first scholarly edition of the Arabic text with a translation and analysis was published—in Germany.[30] Careful scholarly investigation has been rare, given the importance of the document and the impact of the events of 9/11. Government officials, like academics, have also ignored the document. In this book we take a very different approach. We consider that the document is relevant to a full understanding of what happened and to a clarification of crucial issues that remain unsolved. These issues include a consideration of: the instructions in the *Spiritual Manual* in light of Islam; the concept of martyrdom and the occurrence of suicide attacks in Islamic history; the impact of the theology of Usama bin Ladin on the attack; the attackers' definition of the situation of Muslims today and their conviction that they performed a raid (in Arabic *ghazwa*) similar to that of the Prophet when he established Islam as a polity in Medina; the social matrix of the attacks; and the role of Jihad hymns as a means of self-motivation among the Hamburg group. Each of these issues is covered in the following chapters.

2

TRANSLATION OF THE *SPIRITUAL MANUAL*

Tilman Seidensticker, Albrecht Fuess, Moez Khalfaoui, and Hans G. Kippenberg

In this translation,[31] such additions as the numbers of surahs and verses as well as the numbering of paragraphs on pages 2 to 4, appear in square brackets. Words inserted to clarify and improve the English translation appear in round brackets. In the contributions to this volume, we refer to the translation by first giving the number of the 'Stage' (First Stage = page 1; Second Stage = page 2; Third Stage = top of page 3 to end of page 4).

[Page 1]

The Last Night [= First Stage]

1. Mutual pledge to die and renewal of intention.[32] Shaving off excess hair from the body and perfuming oneself. Performing the greater ritual ablution (or: washing oneself/taking a shower).
2. Knowing the plan well from all angles; expecting the enemy to react or resist.
3. Reciting the surahs *al-Tawba* [surah 9] and *al-Anfāl* [surah 8] and considering their meaning and the eternal blessing God has prepared for the believers, (especially) for the martyrs. One of the Prophet's companions said, 'The Messenger of God commanded us to recite them before the raid. We then recited them, gained booty and remained unharmed'.[33]
4. Reminding yourself of unconditional obedience that night, as you will encounter decisive situations that require 100 per cent unconditional obedience. Pull yourself together, make yourself understand, convince yourself and incite yourself to this action.[34] The Most High

has said, 'And obey God, and his Messenger, and do not quarrel together, and so lose heart, and your power depart; and be patient; surely God is with the patient'. [Koran 8:46]

5. Staying awake during the night and imploring in prayer[35] for assistance, strengthening, clear triumph, easing the task and covering us.
6. Reciting abundantly, and know that the best way of recitation is reciting the Noble Koran according to a consensus[36] of the scholars, as far as I know. It is sufficient for us that it consists of the word of the Creator of Heavens and Earth whom you are approaching.
7. Purify your heart, cleanse it from stains and forget or ignore that thing named 'World'. The time of playing is over, and the true appointment has come. How much of our lifetime did we waste! Why don't we use these hours profitably by offering acts pleasing to God and pious deeds?!
8. Be cheerful, because between you and your wedding there is no more than a few moments. Thereupon the happy, God-pleasing life and the eternal blessing in the company of the prophets, the righteous ones, the martyrs and the virtuous ones will begin. How fine are such companions! [Koran 4:69] We ask God for his grace. Be of good cheer because the Prophet 'liked a positive attitude in all his affairs'.[37]
9. Then, when you fall into tribulation, direct your attention towards how you act and how you remain steadfast and recover. And know 'that what has happened to you could not have missed you and what has missed you could not have happened to you'.[38] And also know that this tribulation is sent from God in order to elevate your rank and to atone for your sins. And also know that it won't be long before (the tribulation) will vanish with God's permission. Blessed is he who obtains the great reward from God. The Most High has said, 'Or did you suppose you should enter paradise without God knowing who of you have struggled and who are patient?' [Koran 3:142]
10. And remember the word of God the Most High, 'You were longing for death before you met it; now you have seen it, while you were beholding'. [Koran 3:143] Thereafter remember the saying, 'How often a little company has overcome a numerous company, by God's leave!', [Koran 2:249] and his—he is Most High—word, 'If God helps you, none can overcome you; but if he forsakes you, who then can help you after him? Therefore in God let the believers put all their trust'. [Koran 3:160]

11. Remind yourself and your brothers of the prayers and contemplate what their meaning is: the prayers of the morning and the evening, the prayers of the town and the prayers of (arriving at) a locality and the prayers of meeting the enemy, etc.
12. (Use the magical properties of the Koran by reciting from it and then) spitting[39] on yourself, the suitcase, the clothes, the knife, your equipment, your ID, your f[light] t[icket],[40] your passport, all your papers.
13. Check your weapon before departing and again immediately before departing, and 'each one of you must sharpen his knife in order to relieve his slaughter animal'.[41]
14. Tighten your clothes well. This is the way of the pious forefathers as they used to tighten their clothes prior to battle. Then tighten your shoes well and wear socks so that (your feet) will stick in the shoes and will not slip out of them. All these things are measures we were commanded to follow. 'God is sufficient for us; an excellent Guardian is he'. [Koran 3:173]
15. Perform the ritual morning prayer in a group and think about its reward and thereafter perform the prayers. Do not leave the apartment without having performed the ritual ablution, because the angels will ask (God) to forgive you as long as you are in a state of ritual purity and will pray for you. And recite the word of God the Most High, 'What, did you think that We created you only for sport…?' [Koran 23:115] (Surah 'The Believers')

[Page 2]

Afterwards the Second Stage

[1] When the taxi is taking you to the a[irport],[42] repeat God's name many times in the car by means of the prayer of travel, the prayer of the town, the prayer of (arriving at) a locality, the other prayers.

[2] When you have arrived and you see the a[irport], and when you have left the taxi, recite the prayer of (arriving at) a locality. Whenever you arrive at a locality, recite the prayer of the locality. Smile and be calm, because God is with the believers, and the angels are guarding you without your noticing.

[3] Then recite the prayer, 'God is greater than all his creation…', and say, 'O God, protect us from them as it pleases you', and say, 'O God, we throw you against their throats and we seek refuge in you from their evil', and say, 'O God, put for us "before them a barrier and behind them a barrier and cover them, so they do not see"' [cf.

Koran 36:9], and say, 'God is sufficient for us; an excellent Guardian is he'. [Koran 3:173]

[4] And remember the word of God the Most High, 'Those to whom the people said, "The people have gathered against you, therefore fear them"; but it increased them in faith, and they said, "God is sufficient for us; an excellent Guardian is he".' [Koran 3:173]

[5] Having said so, you will find matters organized [...] because God has promised the following to his servants who say this prayer: 1. a return with God's grace and bounty, 2. no evil will touch them, 3. accordance with the grace of God.

[6] The Most High has said, 'So they returned with blessing and bounty from God, untouched by evil; they followed the good pleasure of God; and God is of bounty abounding'. [Koran 3:174] Consequently, their equipment, their gates[43] and their technology, all of this does neither benefit nor harm except with God's permission.

[7] The believers don't fear that. Only the followers of Satan fear it, who in reality fear Satan and have become his followers—God forbid! Fear is a great act of worship which is permitted to be offered only to God, and he is most worthy of it.

[8] The Most High has said, commenting on these verses, 'That is Satan frightening his friends'. [Koran 3:175] Those who are enchanted by Western civilization are people who have drunk their love and reverence with cold water. They feared their (own) weak, fragile devices. 'Therefore do not fear them; but fear you Me, if you are believers'. [Koran 3:175] Fear is a great act of worship. The followers of God and the believers offer it only to the one and only God in whose hand are all things. Be sure that God will frustrate the guile of the unbelievers as he has said, 'That for you; and that God weakens the unbelievers' guile'. [Koran 8:18]

[9] Then you must recite the [...] prayer, which belongs to the highest ones. It is especially important to do it in such a way that nobody takes notice of you praying *lā ilāha illā llāh*.[44] If you say it a thousand times, nobody should be able to distinguish whether you are silent or invoking God.

[10] Part of the greatness (of this formula used as a prayer) are the Prophet's words, 'Whoever says "There is no God but God" in full belief will enter paradise',[45] or as he may have said it. Concerning this topic, the Prophet has said, 'If the seven heavens and the seven earths were put in one scale-pan and *lā ilāha illā llāh* in the other one, the latter would outweigh the first'.[46]

[11] And you can smile while repeating it; this is accomplished by the greatness of this formula. When considering it, one notices that none of its letters are dotted.[47] This is part of their perfect sublimity since dotted letters are inferior[48] to undotted ones.

[12] In any case, it is sufficient that it is the formula professing the oneness of God (*tawḥīd*) that you have come to raise and to fight under its banner, as the Prophet, his companions and those who followed them bravely did (and will do) until the Day of Judgement.

[Page 3]

[13] Furthermore, don't show traces of confusion or tension, but be happy, cheerful, bright and confident because you carry out an action that God loves and approves. Then, a day will come that you will spend with God's permission with the black-eyed (virgins) in paradise.

[14] And smile in the face of perdition, young man,
since you will soon enter eternal abodes.

[15] Wherever you go and whatever you do, always perform the prayers. God grants his pious servants protection, facilitation, success, strengthening, assistance and everything else.

The Third Stage

[1] When you board the p[lane][49]: The very moment you put in your foot, and even before you really enter it, proceed with the prayer and the prayers, and consider that it is a raid on the path (of God) as the Prophet has said, 'Marching out in the morning and returning in the evening on the path of God is better than this world and what is in it',[50] or how he has said it.

[2] When you step into the p[lane] and take your seat, say the prayers and recite the known prayers we have already mentioned. Busy yourself with uttering God's name and always repeating it.

[3] The Most High has said, 'O believers, whensoever you encounter a host, then stand firm, and remember God frequently; haply so you will prosper'. [Koran 8:45]

[4] When the p[lane] begins to move slightly and heads for the starting position [?],[51] recite the prayer of travel because you are travelling to God the Most High. 'And how blessed is this journey!'

[5] Then you will find (the plane) stopping, and thereafter it will start. This is the moment of the encounter of the two camps. Recite prayers to God as he has stated in his book, 'Our Lord, pour out upon us patience, and make firm our feet, and give us aid against the

people of the unbelievers!', [Koran 2:250] and also, 'Nothing else they said but, "Lord, forgive us our sins, and that we exceeded in our affair, and make firm our feet, and help us against the people of the unbelievers"'. [Koran 3:147]

[6] And God's Prophet said, 'O God, you who have sent down the Book, moved the clouds and defeated the factions,[52] defeat them and make us victorious. O God, defeat them and make them tremble'.[53]

[7] Pray for victory, assistance and the hitting of the target for yourself and for all of your brothers, and don't be afraid. And ask God to grant you martyrdom while you are moving forward and not retreating, persevering and hoping for God's reward.

[8] Then each one of you should prepare himself to fulfil his task in a manner which pleases God. And everyone should grit his teeth as our forefathers used to do before engaging in a battle.

[9] In close combat, strike firmly like heroes who do not wish to return to this world. Exclaim loudly *Allāhu akbar*, because the exclaiming of *Allāhu akbar* instils fright into the unbelievers' hearts. And the Most High has said, 'So smite above the necks, and smite every finger of them!' [Koran 8:12]

[10] And know that the Gardens have adorned themselves with their most distinct garbs and the paradise virgins are calling you, saying, 'O friend of God, come', wearing their nicest clothing.

[11] And when God grants any of you a slaughter, you should dedicate it to father and mother because they have a claim on you. Do not disagree among one another and be absolutely obedient. If you slaughter, rob those you have killed as this is a custom of Muḥammad's, on condition that you don't rob if there is danger of neglecting something more important, such as paying attention to the enemy, his deceptions and attacks. The harm of this would be much greater.

[12] If that is the case,

[Page 4]

the benefit of the action has priority, and (in general) the (interest of the) group has to be given priority over following this custom, because the operation is an obligation to be fulfilled while this (i.e. robbing) is a custom, and the obligatory has to be given priority over the custom.[54]

[13] Do not take vengeance for yourself, but make your strike and everything else for the sake of God. Take for example 'Alī Ibn Abī Ṭālib.[55] When he once fought against an unbeliever, the unbeliever

spat on him. 'Alī then let his sword pause and did not strike him. Only afterwards did he strike him.

[14] After the battle, one of the companions asked him why he had done so, why he had not struck the unbeliever, and first left off and only later struck him. 'Alī answered, 'When he spat on me, I feared I would strike him out of vengeance. Therefore I held my sword', or how he said.

[15] When he had called the intention to mind, he turned to him and struck and killed him.[56] All this means that the human being should prepare his soul in a very short time, and then all he does is for the sake of God.

[16] Afterwards apply [the Prophet's] custom of taking prisoners of war. Take some of them and kill them as the Most High has said, 'It is not for any prophet to have prisoners until he make wide slaughter in the land. You desire the chance goods of the present world, and God desires the world to come; and God is All-mighty, All-wise'. [Koran 8:67]

[17] If everything has come off well, each of you is to pat his brother from the apartment on the shoulder. And in the a[irport] and in the p[lane] and in the c[ockpit][57] (each of you) should remind him that this operation is for the sake of God. And none of you should confuse or disturb his brothers, but make them hopeful, comfort them, remind them and encourage them.

[18] How delightful it would be if one recited some verses from the Koran such as the saying of the Most High, 'So let them fight in the way of God who sell the present life for the world to come…', [Koran 4:74] and, 'Count not those who were slain in God's way as dead…', [Koran 3:169] and other verses.

[19] Or you may also recite (poetry) to them as the forefathers used to recite *rajaz* poetry[58] in the midst of the battle to comfort the brothers and to fill their hearts with calmness and joy.

[20] Do not forget to take some booty, even if it is just a cup or a glass of water you drink from and offer it to your brothers if it is possible.

[21] When the true promise and the zero hour approach, tear your suit and open your chest welcoming death on the path of God.

[22] Always mind God, either by ending with the ritual prayer (*ṣalāt*), if this is possible, starting it seconds before the target, or let your last words be, 'There is no God but God, and Muḥammad is his Prophet'.

[23] After that, God willing, the meeting in the highest paradise will follow through God's mercy.

[24] *When you see the crowds of unbelievers, remember the factions whose number amounted to 10,000 thousand [*sic*] fighters and how God made his believing servants victorious. And the Most High has said, 'When the believers saw the Confederates they said, 'This is what God and his Messenger promised us, and God and his Messenger have spoken truly'. And it only increased them in faith and surrender', [Koran 33:22] and may God bless our prophet Muḥammad and grant him salvation.[59]

3

THE INSTRUCTIONS GIVEN IN THE *SPIRITUAL MANUAL* AND THEIR PARTICULAR INTERPRETATION OF ISLAM

Tilman Seidensticker

1. *A Quantitative Overview of the Instructions*

As a first step, I will determine which types of instructions are given in the text and how much space is devoted to each of them. The distinction between non-religious and religious elements allows us to determine the extent to which we are entitled to speak of the text as a *Spiritual Manual.* Another distinction, namely that between external and internal behaviour, will help us to understand better the specific character of the religious instructions. In practice, a sorting of the various instructions into the four categories resulting from the combinations of these features will always involve a certain degree of arbitrariness, but the overall result is unlikely to change dramatically even if single cases were categorized differently.

The length of the text amounts to approximately 1570 words (Arabic conjunctions and particles consisting of a single letter have not been counted). Exact figures are only given for categories with a very small share; in all other cases, I will give estimated percentages.

The results of this analysis are as follows:

1. Instructions referring to externally visible behaviour of a non-religious character, as might be found in similar papers of any secular or Marxist liberation organization as well, amount to just 67 words, which correspond to a share of a little more than four per cent. Specifically, this category includes the instructions (a) to check the weapon (1/13), (b) to tighten clothes and shoes and to wear socks (1/14), (c) to recite the formula *lā ilāha illā llāh* in a manner that will not be noticed by anyone (2/9), (d) to strike firmly in close combat (3/9), and (e) not to disagree and to be obedient (3/11).

2. Non-religious instructions that aim at an internal preparation for the extreme stress of the upcoming events are similarly rare. The identification of such passages is difficult, because sometimes they have to be isolated somewhat forcibly from their religiously imbued context. If we proceed liberally, the result is 59 words, which equals about four per cent. The following instructions can be allocated to this category: (a) to know the plan well and to be prepared for resistance (1/2), (b) to be unconditionally obedient in a very difficult situation (1/4), (c) to stay steadfast in tribulation (*ibtilā'*, Koranic phrase!, 1/9), (d) not to show nervousness (2/13), and (e) to prepare for the fulfilment of the task (3/8, 'in a manner which pleases God'!).
3. Instructions for religiously imbued, externally visible behaviour, including regular cultic practice, have a slightly larger share; I count 90 words, which equals six per cent. In detail, these are the following statements: the command (a) to shave and wash oneself/to perform ablutions (1/1), (b) to use the magical practice of spitting (1/12), (c) to perform a common morning prayer (*ṣalāt al-ṣubḥ*, 1/15), (d) to leave the apartment only in a state of ritual purity (1/15), and (e) to utter the traditional Muslim battle cry *Allāhu akbar* in order to frighten the enemy (3/9). The order (f) to take captives and to kill them (3/16) must be considered a command referring to a religious act, because a Koranic verse is adduced to legitimize such behaviour. Again, the command (g) to take booty must be understood as a religious command, because it is presented as a Prophetic custom in the first of the two paragraphs in which it is mentioned (3/11; 3/20). The proposal (h) to finish the mission by performing a ritual prayer (*ṣalāt*, 3/22) is strange here; less because this sort of prayer is bound up with certain times of the day than because such a prayer requires much more space than is available in an airplane cockpit.
4. The whole remainder of the text, that is, 86 per cent, is concerned with internal religious preparation for the different phases of the mission.[60] These instructions for a spiritual preparation consist of two types of commands, which are represented roughly equally here: a) commands to recite and b) spiritual arming proper.

1.1. *Commands to Recite*

The texts recommended for recitation are Koranic verses, prayers and—to a lesser degree—poetry. As for reciting from the Koran, the author of the document explains that Koranic verses rank highest among the prayers according to the consensus among religious scholars 'as far as I know' (1/6). Already in the first line he mentions the surahs 9 and 8 as especially suited (1/3); a few lines later he quotes the wording of several Koranic verses as suitable for recitation; and the whole text is interspersed with such quotations until the last page.

The prayers prescribed by the author throughout the text are not identical with the ritual prayer (*ṣalāt*), which is recommended twice (1/15; 3/22); rather, they are petitionary prayers to be formulated freely, or certain supplications with a fixed wording intended for different times or occasions. In principle, a *du'ā'* is a general or specific supplication, whereas a *dhikr* is an utterance that names or describes God. Our text, however, does not draw such a clear distinction (and neither do the classical collections of prayers); in most places *du'ā'* and *dhikr* are used interchangeably. The recommended prayers are sometimes given in full (as, for example, a prayer of Muḥammad's in 3/6). Elsewhere only the content of the supplication is mentioned (for example, asking for assistance, strengthening, etc., in 1/5), and in many instances just short titles are used, such as 'the prayer of travel' (*dhikr al-rukūb*, 2/1) and 'the prayer of (arriving at) a locality' (*du'ā' al-makān*, 2/2). Such prayers, alluded to simply by their names, are known to most contemporary Muslims and are recited loudly or silently on a great variety of occasions.[61]

Besides such prayers, the first part of the Islamic creed (*lā ilāha illā llāh*) is recommended for recitation (2/9). The suggestion that nobody will notice the (quiet) reciting of this formula if it is repeated a thousand times gives an idea of the scale of the repetition involved.

In one instance, the recitation or extemporizing of poetry is recommended as a practice of the 'pious ancestors' (*al-salaf*, 4/19). Possibly this instruction refers to such verses as in 2/14.

1.2. *Spiritual Arming*

Within the second half of the remainder of the text, which deals with spiritual arming, the martyrs' certain admission to paradise figures large. Such allusions can be found from the first lines of the first page ('the eternal blessing God has prepared for the believers, especially for the martyrs', 1/3) to the last lines of page 4 ('the meeting in the highest paradise', 3/23). Altogether, the martyrs' prospect of paradise, including the pleasures with the *houris*, is mentioned 12 times. Although one should be careful not to attach too much importance to this topic in explaining why suicide attacks are planned, its role in the execution of such attacks can hardly be overstated.[62]

Quite numerous are admonitions to reflect: on the meaning of surahs 9 and 8 (1/3), on Koran 2:249 (1/10), on the various prayers (1/11) and on the ritual morning prayer (*ṣalāt*, 1/15). Closely related to that is the instruction to 'consider that it is a raid on the path of God' (3/1).

A last group of instructions aiming at a religious arming is composed of commands to be of good spirit: to purify the heart and to forget this life (1/7), to be cheerful and calm (1/8 [twice]; 2/2), not to be afraid (3/7), and, finally, to welcome death (3/21, accompanied by the external act of tearing one's suit).

In summary, it may be said that the share of non-religious instructions, whether their content is externally visible or to be carried out only mentally, is quite small, amounting to no more than eight per cent. Among the instructions with a religious character, those relating to externally visible behaviour similarly do not figure prominently, since their share does not exceed six per cent. In contrast, the share of those passages of the text that aim at internal religious motivation amounts to 86 per cent. The title *Spiritual Manual*, therefore, seems quite appropriate. Religious arming is achieved by two means: first, the excessive recitation of religious texts and formulae; secondly, motivation by constantly repeated references to the martyrs' blissful future, admonitions to reflect and to gain a positive outlook on the 'way on the path of God'.

2. *The Text's Particular Interpretation of Islam*

The first striking peculiarity of our text is the complete absence of any attempt to justify the mission for which it was composed. There is no allusion to a collective humiliation of Muslims, which is often considered the principal source of Islamist rage; nor is any attempt made to console the perpetrators for the killing of thousands of civilians. The explanation seems to be that both the reason and the justification were self-evident to the addressees of the *Spiritual Manual*.

A second feature worth mentioning is the enormous role assigned to the recitation of prayers (in Arabic *dhikr* and *du'ā'*). Juan Cole has rightly pointed out a resemblance between the repeated prayers recommended in the *Spiritual Manual* and the practices of the Sufis, the Islamic mystics.[63] In fact, the *dhikr* is a means to revere and approach God, and, as such, is common to almost all Sufi orders throughout the ages. Cole also mentions that 'even the Muslim Brotherhood strain of Islamic fundamentalism did not explicitly reject Sufi figures such as al-Ghazali, and there was a Sufi tinge to some Brotherhood texts and practices'. He concludes 'that the text exhibits not so much Sufism as simple common

Islamic spirituality, if put to monstrous uses'. In fact, Ḥasan al-Bannā, founder of the Muslim Brotherhood, left behind a book containing a great number of such prayers for many occasions of daily life, which was published with a preface by his grandson Tariq Ramadan.[64]

Perhaps we can go even further. Figure 2 (next page) shows two pages of a small card with prayers compiled by the Saudi theologian Bin Baz ('Abdal'azīz Ibn 'Abdallāh Ibn Bāz, d. 1999).[65] It was printed in Riyadh and contains numerous prayers for many occasions of daily life, such as entering one's flat, leaving it, putting on a garment, having paid back a debt, etc. We also find the prayers of the morning and the evening and the prayer of the (entering of a) place (*du'ā' nuzūl al-makān*) mentioned here. Among the prayers to be spoken after the ritual prayer (*ṣalāt*), he adduces the formulae *subḥān Allāh* ('God be praised!'), *al-ḥamdu li-llāh* ('thank God'), and *Allāhu akbar* ('God is great'), each to be repeated 33 times. A fourth formula is mentioned to bring the total to one hundred.

Of course, the repeating of prayers is quite common in the Islamic world; normally, the rosary (*subḥa* or *misbaḥa*) is used to facilitate counting. The surprising thing is that the Wahhābī or Salafī cleric Bin Baz recommends such frequent and frequently repeated prayers. Therefore, Cole's assessment could be amended: certain forms of *dhikr* are not only mainstream Islam, but are accepted even in Saudi Arabia, with its strong anti-Sufi tradition.

Two other elements are on the same level as this one: namely, the recommended custom of spitting on one's own person and on important things (after having recited from the Koran) to ensure protection (*nafth*, 1/12), and the role that is assigned to Satan (*al-Shayṭān*) as the reason for disproportionate fear of Western superiority (2/6-8). Both elements are reminiscent of popular religion, which is not normally a prominent trait of radical Islamist thought and propaganda. But while many customs of popular Islam go back to regional pre-Islamic or non-Islamic religions, *nafth* can be traced back to the prophet Muḥammad via Prophetic tradition, and Satan is a figure mentioned in the Koran (as the quotation in 2/8 shows). Therefore, both elements are compatible with the rigorous Wahhābī perception of Islam, which rejects all customs that cannot be proved to go back to Muḥammad and the Koran.

A third strange feature of our text is the observation that the first part of the Islamic creed only contains undotted letters, which for some reason are considered superior to dotted ones (2/11). In this case, there is no way of attributing this opinion to Muḥammad or the Koran, not least because the diacritical dots were introduced a long time after Muḥammad's death (as the undotted script of ancient parchment Korans shows).

بسم الله الرحمن الرحيم

الذكر بعد الصلاة

من عبدالعزيز بن عبدالله بن باز إلى جميع من يراه من المسلمين
من السنة أن يقول المسلم بعد كل فريضة :
« أستغفر الله ... ثلاث مرات »
« اللهم أنت السلام، ومنك السلام، تباركت ياذا الجلال والإكرام » « رواه مسلم برقم ٥٩١ ».
« لا إله إلا الله وحده لاشريك له ، له الملك وله الحمد، وهو على كل شيء قدير، لا حول ولا قوة إلا بالله، لا إله إلا الله ، ولانعبد إلا إياه ، له النعمة وله الفضل وله الثناء الحسن ، لا إله إلا الله مخلصين له الدين ولو كره الكافرون » « رواه مسلم برقم ٥٩٤ » « اللهم لامانع لما أعطيت ولا معطي لما منعت، ولاينفع ذا الجد منك الجد » « رواه البخاري برقم ٨٤٤ ».
ويقول بعد صلاة الفجر وصلاة المغرب مع ماتقدم : « لا إله إلا الله وحده لاشريك له، له الملك وله الحمد يحيي ويميت وهو على كل شيء قدير » عشر مرات « صحيح سنن الترمذي برقم ٢٥٣٤ ».
ثم بعد ذلك يقول : « سبحان الله » ثلاثاً وثلاثين و« الحمد لله » ثلاثاً وثلاثين و« الله أكبر » ثلاثاً وثلاثين ، ويقول تمام المائة : « لا إله إلا الله وحده لاشريك له، له الملك وله الحمد وهو على كل شيء قدير » « رواه مسلم برقم ٥٩٧ ».
ثم يقرأ آية الكرسي: ﴿ الله لا إله إلا هو الحي القيوم لاتأخذه سنة ولانوم له مافي السموات ومافي الأرض من ذا الذي يشفع عنده إلا بإذنه يعلم مابين أيديهم وماخلفهم ولايحيطون بشيء من علمه إلا بما شاء وسع كرسيه السموات والأرض ولايؤوده حفظهما وهو العلي العظيم ﴾ « رواه ابن السني في عمل اليوم والليلة برقم ١٢٦ ».
ثم يقرأ : ﴿ قل هو الله أحد ﴾ ، ﴿ قل أعوذ برب الفلق ﴾ ، ﴿ قل أعوذ برب الناس ﴾ ، وبعد المغرب والفجر يكرر : ﴿ قل هو الله أحد ﴾ و﴿ قل أعوذ برب الفلق ﴾ و﴿ قل أعوذ برب الناس ﴾ « ثلاث مرات هذا هو الأفضل » « انظر صحيح سنن أبي داود برقم ١٣٢٢ ».
وصلى الله على نبينا محمد وعلى آله وصحابه وأتباعه بإحسان إلى يوم الدين

دعاء لبس الثوب : « الحمد لله الذي كساني هذا الثوب ورزقنيه من غير حول مني ولا قوة » « صحيح سنن أبي داود برقم ٤٠٢٣ ».
دعاء دخول المسجد : « أعوذ بالله العظيم وبوجهه الكريم وسلطانه القديم من الشيطان الرجيم »(١) « بسم الله والصلاة »(٢) « والسلام على رسول الله »(٣) « اللهم افتح لي أبواب رحمتك »(٤)
(١) « صحيح سنن أبي داود برقم ٤٦٦ ».
(٢) « رواه ابن السني برقم ٨٨ والحديث حسن ».
(٣) « صحيح سنن أبي داود برقم ٤٦٥ ».
(٤) « رواه مسلم برقم ٧١٣ ».
دعاء الخروج من المسجد : « بسم الله والصلاة والسلام على رسول الله ، اللهم إني أسألك من فضلك » « انظر تخريج روايات الحديث السابق ».
دعاء تعويذ الأولاد : « أعيذكما بكلمات الله التامة من كل شيطان وهامة ومن كل عين لامة » « رواه البخاري برقم ٣٣٧١ ».
دعاء الكرب : « لا إله إلا الله العظيم الحليم ، لا إله إلا الله رب العرش العظيم ، لا إله إلا الله رب السموات ورب الأرض ورب العرش العظيم » .
« رواه مسلم برقم ٢٧٣٠ ».
دعاء الهم والحزن : « اللهم إني أعوذبك من الهم والحزن والعجز والكسل والبخل والجبن وضلع الدين وغلبة الرجال » .
« رواه البخاري برقم ٢٨٩٣ ».
دعاء قضاء الدين : « اللهم اكفني بحلالك عن حرامك وأغنني بفضلك عمن سواك » « صحيح سنن الترمذي برقم ٣٥٦٣ ».
دعاء من استعصب عليه أمر : « اللهم لا سهل إلا ماجعلته سهلاً وأنت تجعل الحزن إذا شئت سهلاً » « رواه ابن حبان في صحيحه برقم ٩٧٠ ».
دعاء كفارة المجلس : « سبحانك اللهم وبحمدك أشهد أن لا إله إلا أنت أستغفرك وأتوب إليك » « صحيح سنن الترمذي برقم ٣٤٣٣ ».

« دار الثبات للنشر والتوزيع - الرياض - شارع السويدي العام شرق النفق
تلفاكس : ٤٢٨٣١٧٢ - هاتف ٤٢٤٢١٧٧

مطبعة دار طيبة - الرياض - ت: ٤٢٨٣٨١٠

Figure 2. *Prayer Card Compiled by Bin Baz.*

A fourth striking trait is the command to take booty, an order that is made twice. In the first mention, it is recommended that the killed persons be robbed because this was the custom of Muḥammad (3/11); in the second instance, the addressees are reminded to take booty (*ghanīma*), be it only a cup of water (3/20). To my knowledge, such a duty to take booty is mentioned nowhere in the jihad chapters of the classical legal works; on the contrary, there we encounter admonitions not to make jihad just for the sake of material gain. Moreover, the concept of an alleged looting ritual appears particularly absurd when it is practised by persons who will die a few minutes later. Perhaps the irrationality of this 'duty' can help us to understand its real aim—probably this task is designed to keep the perpetrators busy and distract them from their imminent deaths.

A fifth conspicuous characteristic is the designation *dhabīḥa* ('slaughter animal, sacrificial victim') used for the enemy who has to be killed (1/13), and the verb *dhabaḥa* ('to slaughter, to sacrifice') to describe this act (3/11). In our text, the aim is clearly to represent killing as a pious deed and thereby to legitimize it. As has been extensively reported of late, cutting a man's throat has been a widespread method of killing since the outbreak of the Algerian civil war, probably because it is both archaic and terrifying. In the course of the hijackings of 11 September, however, the perpetrators are believed to have had no other weapons at their disposal than box-cutters. Therefore, the method of killing was more a matter of practicability than of symbolism. The recommendation in 3/11 to dedicate the slaughter to father and mother is very strange; once more, one is tempted to see this as an attempt to keep the perpetrators occupied.

The sixth and final idiosyncratic feature is the use of legal language in 3/12. The fabricated custom of taking booty is represented as being of secondary importance compared with the success of the mission, and this assessment is based on the rule that 'duties (*wājib*) have priority over custom (*sunna*)'. In 1/6, a claim to some degree of religious expertise was already staked with the mention of the consensus among the scholars (*ijmāʿ ahl al-ʿilm*).

3. *Conclusions*

In April 2002, Yosri Fouda, London bureau chief of the al-Jazeera television network, met Ramzi Binalshibh and Khalid Sheikh Mohammad in Karachi, Pakistan. These two men were the planners of the 9/11 attacks; since then, both have been arrested in Pakistan and are in US detention at an unknown location. Fouda published his recollections of the meeting and the information he obtained in the book *Masterminds of Terror*.[66] In several passages in the book, Abdulaziz al-Omari (= ʻAbdalʻazīz al-ʻUmarī) is mentioned as the author of the *Spiritual Manual*, and Binalshibh told Fouda that the copy published by the FBI was written in al-Omari's handwriting.

Al-Omari was a member of Mohammed Atta's group, which hijacked American Airlines flight 11. Some reliable information on him may be contained in his farewell video, which was edited and published by the notorious al-Saḥāb Institute, the media and propaganda branch of al-Qaeda, after the attacks. An anonymous speaker reports that al-Omari was born in a village near al-Makhwāh (also spelled al-Mikhwāh and al-Mukhwāh) in the Saudi Arabian province al-Bāḥa; al-Makhwāh is about 150 miles to the south of Mecca. Al-Omari's father was a teacher at the Friday mosque in that town. Al-Omari himself studied religious subjects such as Prophetic tradition and Islamic law in the Qasīm province in the north of Saudi Arabia. Nine of his professors are mentioned by name, among them the radical scholar Sulaymān al-ʻAlwān (or al-ʻUlwān), who is said to have been his teacher of Prophetic tradition. Reasons and justifications for the suicide mission, which are completely absent from the *Spiritual Manual*, play an important part in this farewell video.

This information fits Fouda's report about al-Omari's authorship of the *Spiritual Manual* quite well, and I see no reason to doubt that he indeed composed and wrote this document which, in the end, achieved its purpose of preparing and motivating nineteen young men to undertake four suicide missions.

Of course, it is difficult to say which elements of the text were the most effective ones. Nevertheless, I will venture to say that the ring of religious expert knowledge was highly important for the fifteen so-called 'muscles', most of whom came from Saudi Arabia, lacked a good education, and were in their mid-twenties (seven of them were no older than 23).

In my opinion, a second very important feature is the mental distraction by means of intensive recitation of religious texts and formulae. As a heritage of the wars between the central European states and the Ottoman Empire in the sixteenth and seventeenth centuries, German libraries such as the Berlin State Library or the Gotha Research Library own a large number of Turkish–Arabic prayer books in manuscript form which were taken as loot. These books show the enormous role that highly repetitive prayer played in the pastoral care and cultic practice of the Ottoman armies. The suicide attacks on the southern Philippine islands committed during the Muslim resistance to Spanish oppression (on which see

Chapter 4) were usually preceded by intensive reciting of prayers as well. And even in (canonical and non-canonical) Prophetic traditions, the reciting of formulae such as *Allāhu akbar*, *lā ilāha illā llāh*, *subḥāna llāh*, of Koranic verses and of *adhkār* is recommended by the prophet Muḥammad to Muslim warriors. Perhaps the author of the *Spiritual Manual* knew these traditions, but it is also conceivable that he simply transferred a 'civil' practice of Muslim religiosity to the realm of jihad. Be that as it may, the custom of reciting prayers seems to be an element that has no counterpart in Christianity, at least not to a comparable extent.

4

The Religious and Historical Background of Suicide Attacks in the Name of Islam

Tilman Seidensticker

1. *Islamic Norms*

In the eyes of the perpetrators, suicide attacks like those of 9/11 are carried out in accordance with the rules of jihad (religiously motivated warfare). These rules are supposed to provide the justification for the use of violence and to guarantee that the warrior, should he die, attain the status of a martyr (*shahīd*). According to widespread belief, the martyr enters paradise immediately and tastes all conceivable bodily delights. These ideas, however, are inconsistent with Islam's strict prohibition on suicide and on killing non-combatants. On the following pages, I will attempt to show how this contradiction is dealt with, and which interpretation is attached to the concepts of jihad, martyrdom, suicide, and civilian status, both historically and in the present. I must first mention that in the presentation of the various positions, the worldview of a certain group of contemporary Muslims is left out of consideration: the silent minority of secularized, educated Muslims who do not refer exclusively to religious tradition when expressing their views and who do not regard everything as binding which others claim to be hallowed by the Koran and by Prophetic tradition. At present, this group has prominent exponents in several countries, but the general climate restricts them from expressing their views publicly.

In the opinion of most (but not all) medieval jurists, the jihad is a duty that, even without the presence of an external threat, is incumbent on at least a 'sufficient number' of warriors. The notion of a 'sufficient number', however, is quite vague; a small battalion somewhere on the fringes of the Islamic world might theoretically be enough. Moreover, there have been prolonged periods of peaceful coexistence between the Islamic and the Christian worlds during which Muslim rulers ignored this duty and instead proved guardians of flourishing trade with Christian partners. If Muslim territory is attacked, jihad is an individual duty, and if there is no ruler to proclaim it, the individual Muslim may—or rather must—take up arms. Whether in a given situation Muslim territory or the practice of Islam is threatened is a question that in many cases cannot be answered by referring to legal sources; rather, it is a question of political and tactical discretion.

In modern times, the predominant view is that during the lifetime of the prophet Muḥammad, jihad already had a purely defensive character, and accordingly is restricted now to defensive uses. Since the days of Sayyid Quṭb, mastermind of the Egyptian Muslim Brotherhood, who was hanged in 1966, the concept of jihad as an individual duty of each Muslim, even in the absence of a concrete threat from outside, has gained ground in extremist Islamist circles. Quṭb's ideal of a worldwide Islamic supremacy is in accordance with the pre-modern theory of offensive jihad. A wholly new feature is his interpretation of jihad as a duty of every Muslim, not just of a 'sufficient number' of fighters. It is based on Quṭb's conviction that the current condition of Islam in nominally Muslim countries is so disastrous that they are more appropriately referred to as 'heathen' (*jāhilī*) countries with just a small minority of real Muslims. As a first step, these true Muslims may fight the 'heathen' governments and those people who are Muslims in name only, and afterwards the struggle against the West can be taken up. It was Quṭb's firm conviction that this was a process that would ultimately liberate mankind from various forms of slavery. His ideas are still flourishing today. In 1997, 'Abdalmalik al-Barrāk published a monograph of about 350 pages in which he uses his vast range of knowledge in the fields of Koranic exegesis, Prophetic tradition, and Islamic history to make the case that jihad has to be interpreted as offensive.[67] Globalized extremist groups like al-Qaeda skip over the first step of fighting the 'heathen' governments in the Islamic world, because these are difficult to attack, or because Western forces are already present in the Islamic world, or, finally, because the extremists consider the West the real cause of the problems of the Muslim countries.[68]

A peculiarity of the radicals' approach is the idea that jihad can be practised by an individual; this is of primary importance for the phenomenon of suicide attacks. After the invasion of Iraq in March 2003, Muḥammad Sayyid Ṭanṭāwī, Shaykh of Al-Azhar University in Cairo, appealed to Muslims to participate in the jihad against the invaders. In response, 'Iṣām al-'Aryān, a prominent leading member of the Egyptian

Muslim Brotherhood, stated that in a system of institutionalized states, jihad, too, has to be led in an institutionalized way by regular armies only, and that troops made up of volunteers should be employed only in exceptional cases. Despite his view, it can be predicted that the individualized way of jihad will remain the dominant type for the foreseeable future. (A comparable phenomenon from European history is the Spanish civil war from 1936 to 1939, when there were tens of thousands of volunteers from most European countries fighting in the International Brigades.)

Somebody who dies in jihad is a martyr (*shahīd*); according to widespread classical and modern opinion, he ascends to paradise immediately, where (after a previous bodily resurrection) he will have his pleasure with the famous paradise virgins. From early times, however, this view has been in dispute, because the Koran is not entirely unambiguous on this point. Some Prophetic traditions tell us that only the martyrs' souls go immediately to paradise, where they dwell in the shape of green birds (or in the bellies or the crops of green birds). This idea still seems to be common today; a book on those killed in the first Intifada bears the title 'The Green Birds'.[69]

The prohibition against suicide (in Arabic: *intiḥār*) cannot be proven beyond doubt to have its foundation in the Koran.[70] In post-Koranic religious and juridical literature, this prohibition is formulated unambiguously, and it is said to be deeply rooted in contemporary Muslim societies.[71] The tension between this taboo and the ideal of military jihad has been solved in different ways. In the canonical collections of Prophetic tradition there are several strong exhortations to be found against voluntary death. To wish for death, we read, is forbidden; it is even forbidden to long for an encounter with the enemy. The conscious intention to spread God's word is an absolute precondition for becoming a martyr; no one who goes into battle only to gain fame can become one.[72]

In the years since 1983, a series of suicide attacks has prompted Muslim theologians to give their views on this conflict. It seems that high-ranking scholars are more reluctant than low-ranking ones to justify such deeds on the record, whether specifically or in general. The conflict of the Palestinians with Israel is considered to have reached a state of necessity that can outweigh the prohibition on suicide even in the eyes of moderate thinkers. More radical theoreticians lift this ban entirely, arguing that things are going similarly badly in other regions of the Islamic world or that the same state of necessity prevails due to the humiliation and powerlessness of the Muslims in general. In any case, costs are weighed against benefits according to the prevailing political circumstances. Sometimes the proximity of 'martyr operations' to suicide is mitigated by equating the attacker with a single warrior fighting against a superior force. In the last analysis, it is argued, the warrior has no better chance of survival than the man or woman undertaking a 'martyr operation', and jurists from classical times did not raise objections to such an encounter if sufficient damage to the enemy could be expected.[73]

Medieval Islamic jurists almost unanimously regard the killing of civilians as prohibited. Two general exceptions are cases of retaliation against similar acts committed by the enemy, and cases in which it is impossible to hit an important military target without killing non-combatants. Both exceptions can, from the radical Muslims' point of view, serve to justify attacks in which non-combatants are the exclusive targets, and such arguments have in fact been made.[74] Moreover, with regard to civilians from Israel, it has been argued that in Israel nobody can be regarded as a civilian, and that civilians in the United States are responsible for their country's foreign policy and military actions in their capacity as voters and taxpayers. (Regarding the latter argument, Muḥammad Ḥusayn Faḍlallāh, co-founder and spiritual guide of the Hizbullah, stated after the attacks of 9/11 that US citizens are insufficiently informed about their state's foreign policy, and that the attacks were therefore unjustified.)[75]

The classical Islamic norms of warfare and violence are of great importance in the Muslim world to this day. These norms cannot, however, be regarded as a system of standing rules. As everywhere in the world, political, economic and social change produces new interpretations of tradition. The defensive concept of jihad in present mainstream Islam is a striking example, because it is in obvious contradiction to classical theory. As there is room for a more pacifist interpretation, there is also latitude for more radical ideas. Presently, the emergence of a consensus is not discernible. At best one can say that there are widespread reservations about the use of violence against civilians, and that suicide attacks are far from being generally accepted.

2. *Attacks in the Islamic World*

In an excellent monograph, Joseph Croitoru has pointed out the thread that connects the Japanese kamikaze pilots of the Second World War with the Islamist attacks of the past 25 years.[76] In 1971, a splinter group of the Japanese Red Army (JRA) left Japan for Lebanon, where an 'Arab Red Army' was founded in cooperation with the 'Popular Front for the Liberation of Palestine'. At Lod Airport near Tel Aviv, three Japanese members of the JRA committed a massacre on 30 May 1972, using machine guns and hand grenades. Twenty-six people, most of them Christian pilgrims from Puerto Rico, were killed and about 80 injured. One of the perpetrators survived and later expressed his deep shame for not having been killed. Numerous suicide attacks, carried out by leftist Palestinian nationalists between 1974 and 1978, were doubtless inspired by this bizarre event. These Palestinian attacks, in turn, paved the way for the attacks that shook Lebanon between 1981 and 1987. It is only in this latter wave that the religious element was brought into play.

This new feature was introduced by Shia theologians and by Ayatollah Khomeini's politics. As a reaction to the Iraqi Baath Party's takeover of power in 1963 and the ensuing relentless persecution of religious (and other) opponents, the Shiite ulama in the holy city of Najaf, led by Ayatollah Muḥammad Bāqir al-Ṣadr, became increasingly radicalized. Within the Twelver Shia, martyrdom had always been a central aspect of religion, but the attitude had been to revere martyrs of former centuries, above all the third Imam Ḥusayn, not to imitate them in reality. In Najaf, and in Iran as well, a decidedly activist interpretation developed in the 1960s.[77] Immediately after the Iranian revolution of 1979, Khomeini institutionalized this concept by founding an organization that became known as 'Basij'. It was composed of male minors of 12 to 16 years of age; their total number is said to have exceeded 300,000.[78] During the Iraqi–Iranian war, beginning in 1980, they were used as 'minesweepers' and cannon fodder; there are reports of more than 20,000 boys killed during a single day.[79] Paradise was of primary importance in the motivation of these minors.

The first suicide attack proper with a 'religious' background was executed in Beirut on 15 December 1981, when a car bomb was detonated in front of the Iraqi embassy, causing the deaths of 61 people. It seems to have been organized by a Shiite group, either by Amal or Hizbullah[80] or, more probably, the Islamic Da'wa Party, formed in Baghdad in the late 1950s, with Muḥammad Bāqir al-Ṣadr playing a prominent role.[81] From 1982 to 1985, the Iranian-sponsored Hizbullah carried out about two dozen suicide attacks against US, French and Israeli military targets in Lebanon. (Secular organizations such as the Syrian Social-Nationalist Party adopted this method from 1985 onwards. They, too, like the Palestinians in the 1970s, attached the label of martyrdom to these attacks, but paradise was not mentioned as an incentive.)

Suicide attacks as a means of political strategy moved back from Lebanon to (Sunni) Palestine as late as 1993, this time including the strong religious emphasis that was given to them by Hizbullah. After the mid-1990s, the phenomenon spread to Pakistan in the east and Algeria in the west. Nevertheless, before 9/11 it was used primarily in the geographical vicinity of the struggle for Palestine.

When the history of suicide attacks within the Islamic world is discussed, the Assassins are inevitably mentioned. This group, which should more correctly be called Nizārīs, carried out countless attacks on minor and major Sunni dignitaries and officials and on crusaders between AD 1090 and 1200. Normally the attackers died in the course of these assaults, in which daggers were the usual weapons. The phenomenon can be traced to the radical heterodox Ismā'īlī (or Sevener Shiite) belief and their political ambitions, which lacked a sufficient territorial base. Because of the Assassins' heretical odour, they are unsuited as historical models for both modern Sunni and Shiite suicide attackers.

The same holds true for the Kharijites, another heterodox group that emerged during the caliphate of 'Alī (r. AD 656-661). Split up into numerous subgroups, they exercised political control in parts of the Arabian Peninsula and Iran in the second half of the seventh century. In their confrontation with the Umayyad central power, they displayed a death-defying fighting spirit. From the numerous poems handed down from them, we know that the promise of paradise was a central element in their motivation.[82] This latter fact offers an instructive parallel to modern times, but the sheer desperation of their way of fighting is different from the sure expectation of death connected with the use of explosives worn around one's body or hidden in one's own car.

Three waves of attacks executed by Muslims against European colonial occupiers have a greater similarity to suicide attacks proper. These attacks were reported from south Asia and southeast Asia between the eighteenth and the early twentieth centuries. The first wave began in the middle of the eighteenth century on the Malabar coast (today Kerala, in southwest India); the last of these incidents in Malabar happened as recently as the beginning of the twentieth century. The background of the attacks on Europeans is the military presence of first the Portuguese and later the British, and the takeover of commerce by Europeans who acted with unmasked brutality and who threatened and destroyed the economic and cultural integrity of the Muslim minority in India.[83]

The second wave took place in Atjeh, the northwest part of Sumatra, which was subdued by the Dutch between 1873 and 1908. During this campaign, according to Dutch reports, about ten per cent of the 700,000 Muslim inhabitants were killed. Only towards the end of this 35-year colonial war, when the chieftains of small areas had surrendered to the Dutch, did the religious scholars organize the individual jihad, carried out by means of suicide attacks. Between 1910 and 1937, more than 120 cases of 'Atjeh-moord' were carried out (the term has since then been a Dutch designation for suicide attack).

The third wave occured in the southern Philippines (Mindanao and Jolo). As in Atjeh, this episode followed the breakdown of local power, in this case following the Spanish offensive in the 1870s. From the beginning of their presence in the Philippines in the sixteenth century, the Spanish had pursued an extremely aggressive policy against Islam, forcing Muslims to embrace Christianity, and destroying numerous mosques and other holy places. The Muslim attackers, carrying out their assaults by running amok with a knife, inflicted heavy losses; they were called 'juramentados', that is, men who had made a vow to kill as many enemies as possible before their own sure deaths by the hands of the attacked ones, who were usually superior in number and arms. After the United States had taken over power in the Philippines from the Spanish in 1898, they pursued a much more liberal policy towards the Moros, but nevertheless had to deal with ongoing suicide attacks.

3. *An Affinity of Suicide Attacks and Islam?*

In the preceding section, we encountered a considerable number of suicide attacks or comparable acts launched by Muslims. There are some elements in Islamic tradition that might support the notion of there being a connection between Islam and self-annihilating violence. The doctrine of warfare for the spread of Islam and the promise of paradise for all those who are killed during this enterprise, both of which go back to the prophet Muḥammad and the Koran, can be adduced as such elements. Another important and perhaps unique feature is the Muslims' consciousness of being part of a community that extends over two continents, that has a strong feeling of solidarity, and that is threatened by continuous Western aggression under the auspices of the Jewish and Christian religions. A last point in this list of elements potentially favoring the tactical means of suicide missions is a comparatively high degree of independence on the part of the religious scholars; acquisition of religious authority is normally not bound to the completion of institutionalized courses of instruction. On the contrary, the most influential (re-)thinkers of Islam in the last century were autodidacts. Lack of central religious authority is a factor of primary importance in several waves of attacks in the Islamic world (Atjeh, southern Philippines, and the Near East since 1982).

Nevertheless, to claim an affinity between Islam and suicide attacks, one must first consider the fact that for Sunni Arab Islam there is no single instance proving this assumption in the almost fourteen centuries of Islamic history before the year 1993. Consider also the 'Black Tigers', a special unit of the LTTE (Liberation Tigers of Tamil Eelam), based in the north and east of Sri Lanka, who have carried out between 100 and 200 suicide attacks since 1987.[84] The Tamils of Sri Lanka are Hindu. During World War II, the Japanese air force is said to have flown about 4000 kamikaze missions.[85] An asymmetrical distribution of power (man-power, territory and other resources, such as money and fuel) obviously plays a role. Another factor might be a mentality that puts more emphasis on the welfare of the community as a whole than on the interests of the individual. The criterion of community support has been brought into the discussion by Kalyvas and Sánchez-Cuenca, who write:

> In addition, we have identified the set of organizations that appear most likely to resort to SMs [= suicide missions], using a hypothesis positing a U-shaped relationship between strategy and support. Organizations that act independently of the community in whose name they act, such as nineteenth-century anarchists, and organizations that are firmly grounded in their community like Hamas or LTTE, may resort to extreme tactics, including SMs. In contrast, organizations that depend crucially on the support of some community but whose actual degree of support is weak, like ETA and IRA, face higher costs from launching SMs: they know that such extreme tactics will provoke a decrease in support and are, therefore, likely to refrain from them.[86]

In a sub-chapter on 'Long-term defensive responses' to suicide missions, Ami Pedahzur (University of Texas, University of Haifa) writes:

> In the majority of the cases (Lebanon, Palestine, Sri Lanka, Turkey, Chechnya), the basic demand of these populations was to be free in their homelands. To be sure, in many instances, this demand was shrouded in clerical rhetoric but religious motivation should be considered only secondary to the main grievances. Hence, it could be assumed that once some of the aggrieved populations' demands are met or, at least, a point is reached where the injured party believes its adversaries are upfront and ready to compromise, its incentive to support the organization dispatching suicide terrorists will diminish.[87]

Although some might call these remarks a truism, and although their applicability to attacks such as 9/11 is limited, one cannot escape the impression that Pedahzur's insight does not rank highly in the thinking of some of those powers that have been the targets of suicide attacks.

5

JIHAD AND CHANGING TIMES: THE POLITICAL THEOLOGY OF USAMA BIN LADIN AND HIS DECLARATIONS OF WAR

Thomas Scheffler

1. *Killers without a Cause?*

Who destroyed the Twin Towers of New York's World Trade Center? Watching the 9/11 attacks on their TV screens, many commentators assumed that the perpetrators were 'apocalyptic' or 'nihilistic' minds with an almost visceral hatred of Western civilization and a contempt for earthly politics. In his address to the Congress on 20 September 2001, President Bush explained: 'They hate our freedoms—our freedom of religion, our freedom of speech, our freedom to vote and assemble and disagree with each other... These terrorists kill not merely to end lives, but to disrupt and end a way of life'.[88] Four weeks later he added that the people whom America was fighting in her 'new war against terror and against evil' were 'people who have no country, no ideology; they're motivated by hate'.[89]

Almost immediately after 11 September, the US government accused al-Qaeda and Usama bin Ladin of having masterminded the attacks. Convincing the American public that Bin Ladin and his people were haters without a political cause was relatively easy as long as media attention focused almost exclusively on the hypnotic images of the attack without putting them into context. No organization claimed responsibility for the attacks, and in the absence of any political communiqué the only available document, the so-called 'Letter of Mohammed Atta', a spiritual manual for the mental preparation of suicide hijackers, became temporarily one of the main keys to al-Qaeda's mental world. This was a problematic approach because the personal motives of suicide terrorists are not necessarily the same as the strategic rationale of the *organization* that 'employs' them.[90] Not surprisingly, the first thing discovered by a journalist who had read the document was that 'it's almost totally unpolitical. There's…not a word about Israel, Palestine, global capitalism or any of the other issues that might be expected to concern terrorists'. And the fact that the letter quoted several verses from the Koran's militant ninth surah (*al-Barā'a* or *al-Tawba*) seemed a sufficient basis on which to surmise that the hijackers had 'a lot in common with the Armageddon cults that appear from time to time on the fringes of all religions'.[91]

It is important to recall that by autumn 2001 plenty of information was already available that could have easily shown that al-Qaeda and Bin Ladin actually *did* have a political ideology and that their activities were framed by a long-term strategy.[92] Bin Ladin's activities had been monitored by Western security agencies for several years. Since January 1996, the CIA had a special research unit for gathering intelligence on him.[93] He had been considered dangerous enough for the United States to bomb his camp in Afghanistan, on 20 August 1998, with seventy-five cruise missiles, each worth $750,000.[94] Bin Ladin himself had not tried to keep his views secret. His two declarations of war—the 'Declaration of Jihad against the Americans occupying the two holy places'[95] and the so-called 'Fatwa' statement of the 'World Islamic Front for Jihad against Jews and Crusaders'[96]—had been published in the London-based daily *al-Quds al-'Arabī* in 1996 and 1998 respectively. Apart from his presence in the Muslim media, he had also given interviews to prominent western journalists such as Robert Fisk (*The Independent*, 1993, 1996, 1997), Scott MacLeod (*Time*, 1996), Peter Arnett (*CNN*, 1997), and John Miller (*ABC*, 1998).[97] Shortly before and during the US invasion of Afghanistan in October 2001, al-Qaeda's leadership dramatically increased its appearances on Arab satellite TV in order to mobilize Muslim solidarity and justify the 9/11 attacks.[98] Finally, with the loss of its safe havens in Afghanistan, the organization and its sympathizers turned to the Internet and tried to compensate for the weakening of its central command structures by an enormous output of ideological statements and propaganda videos, making it hard to ignore the fact that its coherence and its capacity to recruit new followers were now mainly rooted in its ideology and did not necessarily depend on one center or one leader who could easily get killed.[99]

Many of these documents were already available on the Internet in 2001 and 2002, and the most important of them have been published in more carefully edited anthologies.[100] Read together they permit the conclusion that al-Qaeda is not an 'otherwordly' apocalyptic Armageddon cult that seeks to destroy the world or which waits for the next world.

Rather, al-Qaeda is an organization with a long-term 'innerwordly' vision (the establishment of an Islamic state in *this* world), a main mid-term goal (the expulsion of infidel powers from Muslim territory), and a number of short-term objectives, most notably the worldwide mobilization of the Muslim *umma*—aims that the organization pursues by a multi-frontal strategy that uses 'martyrdom operations' not as a means in itself, but as one tactic among others.

2. *Bin Ladin's Discourse*

An outline of Bin Ladin's public discourse, condensed from the many statements released by him and his associates before and during 2001, reveals a pattern that may be reduced to sixteen propositions in four basic steps which I have labeled 'diagnosis', 'solution', 'means', and 'available resources'.

2.1. *Diagnosis*

1. Bin Ladin's texts abound with lists of Muslim *grievances*: Muslim lands are invaded, occupied, and plundered by infidels, and Muslim civilians are killed in great numbers all over the world. His 1996 'Declaration of Jihad' refers to Bosnia, Burma, Chechnya, Eritrea, Ethiopia (Ogaden), India (Assam), Iraq, Kashmir, Lebanon, Palestine, the Philippines, Saudi Arabia, Somalia, Tajikistan, and Thailand (Pattani). Later pronouncements also include Afghanistan, East Timor, Egypt, and Sudan. The countries explicitly mentioned vary from statement to statement. References to Arab countries, however, especially to Palestine and Iraq, appear in all of them. As Peter Bergen astutely remarks, these grievances are political and not cultural: 'he does not rail against the pernicious effects of Hollywood movies, or against Madonna's midriff, or against the pornography protected by the U.S. constitution'.[101]
2. The 'crimes' (*jarā'im*) committed against the Muslims in their lands constitute not only 'a clear proclamation of war [*i'lān ṣarīḥ li-l-ḥarb*] on God, his messenger, and the Muslims'; they are also attributable to one single cause: a worldwide 'Zionist-American' or 'Jewish-Crusader' aggression against Islam and the Muslims.[102]
3. The present governments in the Muslim lands are unable or unwilling to protect the believers and in some cases (most notably Saudi Arabia) even consented to the occupation of their lands by US forces.

4. Attempts by religious, economic, and other leaders to rectify this deplorable state of affairs by way of peaceful consultation have come to nothing. Righteous religious scholars and missionaries have been silenced, killed, or arrested. The people who replaced them are weak or corrupt and cannot be trusted.
5. On the international level, all peaceful remedies have failed. Referring to the UN's role in the conflicts over Palestine, Iraq, Kashmir, Chechnya, East Timor, and Somalia, Bin Ladin holds that 'No Muslim, nor anyone in his right mind, should appeal to it [the United Nations] under any circumstances. It is merely an agent of this crime by which we are massacred daily and which it does nothing to stop'. Earlier in the same statement Bin Ladin says: 'Those who refer our tragedies today to the United Nations, and want us to resolve them through it, are hypocrites who deceive God and His Prophet and those who believe'.[103]

2.2. *Solution*

6. Considering that all peaceful remedies have failed, armed struggle remains the only solution. But since most governments in the Muslim world are unable or unwilling to wage war against the aggressors, armed jihad has become *farḍ 'ayn*, that is, a personal religious duty for every individual Muslim.
7. The aim of this jihad is a *defensive* one, namely, to make the enemy's armies 'leave all the territory of Islam [*kull arḍ al-islām*], defeated, broken, and unable to threaten any Muslim'.[104] In a more precisely worded statement, al-Qaeda's spokesman Sulaymān Abū Ghayth warned the USA and its citizens that:

   > These storms [of hijacked airplanes] will not calm until you retreat defeated in Afghanistan, stop your assistance to the Jews in Palestine, end the siege imposed on the Iraqi people, leave the Arabian Peninsula, and stop your support for the Hindus against the Muslims in Kashmir.[105]

8. Since many Muslim rulers are presently cooperating with Western powers, the *mujāhidūn* should be careful to *avoid internal war among Muslims* on the Arabian Peninsula. An internal war would exhaust the human, economic, and financial resources of the Muslims, destroy the country's infrastructures, divide its society, and destroy the oil industries of the 'Islamic Gulf' which constitute 'a great Islamic wealth and a large economical power essential for the soon to be established Islamic state, with God's permission' (*li-dawlat al-Islām al-qādima bi-idhn Allāh*). An

inter-Arab war might also lead to the territorial partition of Saudi Arabia, especially the annexation of its northern part by Israel. By and large, its outcome would be controlled by the US forces stationed on the Arabian Peninsula.[106]

2.3. *Means*

9. Due to the military superiority of the enemy, conventional warfare should be avoided at the present moment. Instead a guerilla war should be waged based on 'fast moving light forces that work under complete secrecy'.[107]
10. The main obligation for every Muslim in this guerilla war is 'to kill the Americans and their allies—civilians and military [*madaniyyīn wa-'askariyyīn*]'—and to 'seize their money' wherever and whenever it is possible.[108] This controversial ruling (*ḥukm*) was absent in Bin Ladin's 1996 declaration of war. It was added in 1998, probably due to the influence of Ayman al-Ẓawāhirī,[109] who co-signed the Fatwa declaration of the 'World Islamic Front'. Several, sometimes contradictory, reasons have been given by Bin Ladin to justify it. While admitting that 'Our Prophet Muḥammad was against the killing of women and children',[110] Bin Ladin argued that the killing of civilians in warfare is permissible under Islamic law under certain circumstances, most notably in order to (i) *retaliate* for the killing of Muslim civilians,[111] (ii) *deter* the enemy from continuing to kill Muslim civilians,[112] and (iii) achieve a higher military goal that cannot be achieved without harming civilians, even if Muslim prisoners are among them.[113] US civilians, in addition, were not eligible for the status of 'innocent civilians' because they elected their government, paid taxes and, hence, were co-responsible for their nation's politics.[114]
11. Expanding the theatre of defensive jihad to the whole planet is a genuine part of the guerilla strategy proposed by Bin Ladin and his associates. For his lieutenant Ayman al-Ẓawāhirī, it reflects the defeats inflicted on violent Islamist movements by US-supported governments in the Middle East:

> It is clear...that the Jewish–Crusade alliance will not give us time to defeat the domestic enemy, then declare war against it thereafter. Therefore, to adjust to this new reality we must prepare ourselves for a battle that is not confined to a single region, one that includes the apostate domestic enemy and the Jewish-Crusade external enemy.[115]

On the level of Bin Ladin's discourse, however, the main justification for moving the battle to the enemy's ground is to convince US citizens that they won't enjoy security if there is no security for Muslims in the Muslim world:

> I swear by God Almighty Who raised the heavens without effort that neither America nor anyone who lives there will enjoy safety until safety becomes a reality for us living in Palestine and before all the infidel armies leave the land of Muḥammad.[116]

12. Invoking the authority of Ibn Taymiyya (d. 1328), Bin Ladin also argues that in case of emergency, Muslims are permitted to accept the help of fighters whose intention (*niyya*) is not pure, that is, people who are fighting for personal gain or 'do not observe some of the rules and commandments of Islam'.[117] This indicates that, at least in the 1990s, the first priority of Bin Ladin's politics was not religious purity but combat effectiveness.
13. Armed struggle, however, is not the only form of defensive jihad. According to Bin Ladin, an economic boycott of American goods, too, should be an important part of it, especially for those who cannot join the armed struggle for whatever reason.[118] His marked interest in the economic damage inflicted on the United States by the 9/11 attacks[119] makes it quite clear that, for him, these attacks were also meant to weaken the aggressive potential of the enemy: '...so when their economy is depleted they will be too busy with each other to be able to enslave poor peoples'.[120]

2.4. *Available Resources*

14. The most precious *human* resource for implementing this strategy is the availability of a generation of young devoted fighters in whose mind the myth of the superpowers' omnipotence has already been destroyed—fighters who are not afraid of dying, prefer an honorable death to life in humiliation, and are longing for jihad and martyrdom.
15. As of 1996, the most important *geopolitical* resource available to the *mujāhidūn* was 'a safe base...in the high Hindu Kush mountains in Khurasan, where—by the Grace of Allah—the largest infidel military force of the world [= the Soviet Union] was destroyed and the myth of the superpower withered in front of the Mujahideen cries of Allahu Akbar'.[121] Referring to Afghanistan by the antiquated name of *Khurāsān* invokes memories of the eighth-century Abbasid revolution—a movement that started from what was then called Khurāsān, that is, the regions east of western Persia, and ushered in a renewal of the Islamic caliphate.

16. The most important resource of the *mujāhidūn*, however, is a *cosmological* one. Numerous explicit and implicit Koranic references in Bin Ladin's discourse emphasize that it is God who will protect the righteous who strive in his path, and that nothing can happen to them unless it is preordained by God, and that God's signs in contemporary history promise victory to the believers.

3. *Interpretations*

Bin Ladin's discourse has provoked contradictory interpretations. Some pundits argue that it does not represent a political ideology, but rather veils an 'apocalyptic' or 'nihilistic' drive to fight (Western) civilization, whatever the political or theological pretexts.[122] Others suspect an ideological background in religious apocalypticism.[123] Still others maintain that it is a political ideology, namely, a totalitarian one indebted to the most prominent Islamist ideologue of the twentieth century, Sayyid Quṭb (1906–1966).[124] And some see it as a kind of anti-colonial nationalism in Islamic disguise.[125]

3.1. *Bin Ladin's Islamism: a Case of Apocalypticism?*

There is no doubt that Usama bin Ladin is a deeply religious man with a sense of divine providence and the transcendental dimensions of human life: he was proud to tell journalists that his father, before his death in 1967, had been involved, as a building contractor, in major construction works at the holy mosques of Mecca, Medina, and Jerusalem (the three holiest places of Islam), and sometimes had even managed to pray in all three mosques in one single day.[126] Bin Ladin himself told Robert Fisk in 1993 that his war years in Afghanistan had shaped his personal experience of the *sakīna*, the divine tranquillity that God sends down upon His followers to support them in danger and grant them victory.[127] Like many of his companions, he believes in providential dreams.[128] Bin Ladin's official statements abound with references to the Koran and the Sunna,[129] and 'Abd al-Bārī 'Aṭwān, editor-in-Chief of *al-Quds al-'Arabī*, who interviewed him in November 1996 in Tora Bora, recalls that no tape recordings were allowed because Bin Ladin had been afraid of making grammatical or theological mistakes that might be used against him.[130]

Given Bin Ladin's eagerness to speak about religious-political issues, it is all the more significant that his public statements are rather silent on the classic themes of Islamic apocalyptic thought, such as the Mahdī, the Dajjāl, Ya'jūj wa-Ma'jūj, the final descent of 'Īsā Ibn Maryam, and so on.[131] Nor do we find any allegoric or numerological speculations about the nearness of 'the Hour'. True, in several statements Bin Ladin is referring to a *ḥadīth* according to which 'the Hour' will not come until the Muslims fight the Jews and kill them and that the rocks and trees behind which the Jews will try to hide on that day will say: 'O Muslim, O Servant of Allah! There is a Jew behind me, come and kill him!'[132] However, the major function of this *ḥadīth* in Bin Ladin's discourse is not to announce the imminence of the Hour or to proclaim man's ability to hasten its coming by killing Jews. Rather, its rhetorical purpose is to construe and dramatize anti-Jewish hatred by emphasizing that (i) enmity between Muslims and Jews is so deep that it will continue until the end of the world; (ii) therefore, Muslims should not make peace with Jews today; and (iii) the final victory of the Muslims over the Jews is as sure as the End of the world. The belief that, one day, this world will end is indeed a crucial part of Islamic orthodoxy; but the Koran confirms that it is unknown to man whether 'the Hour' is near or far (7:187; 21:109; 67:25-26) and that a day in the sight of the Lord is like a thousand years (32:5) or even 50,000 years (70:4).

If there is any genuinely religious diagnosis of our times in Bin Ladin's thought, it is not the apocalyptic expectation that the *end* of the world is coming soon, but rather that we are living at a charismatic turning point of world history at which God seems to be resolved to profoundly *change* the course of events in favor of the believers. Bin Ladin read the Soviet evacuation of Afghanistan (1988/89) and the subsequent break-up of the Soviet Empire (1991) as a divine encouragement to continue, with God's help, the jihad, in order to defeat the next superpower, the USA, and establish the caliphate of the Islamic *umma*.[133] Compared to God's power, the superpowers of this world are just 'paper tigers',[134] and America is, in Bin Ladin's terminology, even 'the Hubal of the age'.[135] All in all, this diagnosis of the present age has much in common with the ideology of the first Christian Crusade, when Pope Urban II (1088–1099) read the capture of Toledo by Alfonso VI (1085) and the Norman conquest of Sicily (1060–1090) as signs of God's will to change the course of history and encourage Christians to purify themselves from their sins by recapturing Jerusalem.[136]

3.2. *A Case of 'Quṭbian Terrorism'?*

Several experts stress the 'Quṭbian' character of Bin Ladin's discourse.[137] Karen Armstrong even suggests that Bin Ladin's activities should be characterized as 'Qutbian terrorism'.[138] Whatever Quṭbian influences there are on Bin Ladin's thought, it is important to bear in mind that his public statements before September 11 differed from Quṭb's in at least three major aspects.

First, Quṭb explicitly *rejected* the idea of defensive jihad. For him, the duty to wage violent jihad existed irrespective of whether Muslims were attacked or not, because it was rooted in the mission of Islam to 'liberate' mankind from the rule of man-made law.[139] Bin Ladin's official statements, however, focus precisely on the necessity of *defensive* warfare and, thus, are much more in tune with mainstream Arab nationalism and mainstream Muslim Just War theory than with Quṭb's permanent jihad.

Second, Quṭb became famous for his diagnosis that the contemporary Muslim societies were in a state of pagan ignorance (*jāhiliyya*)—an idea that many of his followers in the Muslim world used to accuse their rulers (and sometimes also their co-citizens) of being unbelievers who had to be fought and, if necessary, killed as apostates. 'Qutbism', in other words, stood for (i) prioritizing jihad against the 'near enemy' at home and (ii) the practice of *takfīr*, the excommunication of other Muslims by declaring them infidels (*kuffār*). Bin Ladin's ideology, however, inspired by the success of the Afghan liberation war (1979–1989), prioritized (i) defensive jihad against the main external enemy ('Jews and Crusaders') and was (ii) rather reluctant to practice open *takfīr* against other Muslims in order to preserve Muslim *unity* against the external enemy.[140]

Third, Quṭb is famous for his efforts to conceptualize Islam as a *system*[141]—an approach that has led some critics to liken his thought to Marxism–Leninism.[142] In contrast to Quṭb's intellectual approach, al-Qaeda displays an amazing *pragmatism*, a readiness to adapt to changing local circumstances and to tolerate a considerable degree of ideological diversity in its ranks.[143] It is, for example, obvious that the politics of Abū Muṣ'ab al-Zarqāwī (1966–2006) in Iraq—his aggressive hostility towards Shiite Muslims and his indiscriminate killings of Muslim civilians—differed from the ideology exposed in Bin Ladin's two declarations of war of 1996 and 1998. Nevertheless, in December 2004 Bin Ladin accepted Zarqāwī as 'Emir' of al-Qaeda's Iraqi branch.[144] An organization that works to unleash a multi-local, multi-ethnic global jihad against a far more powerful enemy probably has no other choice than to grudgingly accept as a fact of life not only different ways of waging war, but also co-fighters with questionable motives.

4. *Jihad between Practice and Purity*

Although Bin Ladin's two declarations of war, especially the one of 1998, shocked many observers, the political theology exposed in them was much less radical, exclusive, and systematic than Quṭb's. This lack of theological rigor reflected the group's basic historical experiences. Al-Qaeda was not a sectarian club of theologians but a network of activists who believed in the transforming power of practical jihad. The organization's terror operations have been compared to the 'Propaganda of the Deed' of nineteenth-century European anarchists,[145] but it is equally important to note how important these operations were for the internal integration of the network, too: the Islamist volunteers who have flocked to Afghanistan since the 1980s came from many countries and were rooted in different ethnic, sectarian, and political traditions.[146] Imposing a uniform standard of theological purity on this heterogeneous blend of strong-willed men might instead have escalated the tensions and rivalries between them and, in the end, prevented them from making any constructive contribution to jihad at all. Bin Ladin's first mentor, Sheikh 'Abdallāh 'Azzām (1941–1989), was famous for convincing people that practical jihad was more important than theoretical hair-splitting. His followers admired him for having 'no problems with anybody [among the volunteers]. He always says stop speaking and let's do, let's work, stop fighting, then serve the name of the organization. Serve what the organization comes to serve: the cause'.[147]

This pragmatic attitude seemed to work rather successfully in Afghanistan. Like his mentor, Bin Ladin used to quote authorities from various Sunni law schools,[148] use mainstream Islamic terminology and imagery, and oppose self-destructive sectarianism. For instance, Bin Ladin did not approve of the excesses of the Algerian Armed Islamic Group (GIA, *al-Jamā'a al-islāmiyya al-musallaḥa*), which, in the mid-1990s, had slipped into a paranoid *takfīr* policy that treated anyone as an infidel who didn't support the shrinking group. It is significant that al-Qaeda's Algerian affiliate, the Salafi Group for Preaching and Combat (GSPC, *al-Jamā'a al-salafiyya li-l-da'wa wa-l-qitāl*) broke with the GIA in 1998 because of the latter's indiscriminate killing of Muslim civilians.[149]

It remains an open question how al-Qaeda's political theology would have developed under conditions of long-term defeat and persecution. In any case, before 2001 the organization's pragmatic philosophy was based on the confident expectation that it could help defeat the USA as successfully as the USSR had been defeated in Afghanistan. However, following its own defeat in Afghanistan in 2001, al-Qaeda underwent an unprecedented ideologization, including an increase in both the number and strength of aggressive statements against Muslim 'hypocrites', 'apostates', and 'traitors'. The large-scale killings of Muslim civilians by fighters of Zarqāwī's al-Qaeda organization in Iraq invoke the spectre of the Algerian civil war. In the end, it might be only the decentralized character of the global Jihadist network that might shield it against the growing sectarianism of some of its local cells.[150]

6

DEFINING THE PRESENT SITUATION OF MUSLIMS AND RE-ENACTING THE PROPHET'S *GHAZWA*S

Hans G. Kippenberg

1. *The Meaning of an Action Distinct from the Motives of the Actor*

Knowing that the *Spiritual Manual* was in the hands and minds of the four attacking teams enables us to reconstruct how the attackers understood their action. In addressing this issue I would like to follow sociologists who distinguish the motivations of an actor from the meaning of his/her action. Max Weber in particular emphasized the difference. According to Weber, 'action (including intentional omission and acquiescence) is always intelligible behaviour towards objects, behaviour whose "actual" or "intended" *subjective meaning* may be more or less clear to the actor, whether consciously noted or not'.[151] Because any practical attitude towards the world is mediated by 'meaning', and because 'meaning' is often shaped by religious worldviews and ethics, 'meaning' is different from the personal motivation of the actor, although it is part of his subjective acting. To differentiate this type of meaning from personal motives, Weber coined the notion of 'subjective meaning'. However, since the meaning of an action has to be recognized by others, an actor cannot invent it ad hoc but depends on a stock of available meanings applicable to action. Even if an actor is not able to explicate it, 'meaning' remains part of his/her social transactions and can be retrieved by tracing the historical genealogy of actions.

According to this approach, the motives that led 19 young men to commit suicide in the September 11 attacks were different from the meaning they (and others) attributed to their action. The motives may be quite diverse and need to be explored for each individual separately.[152] For the three members of the Hamburg group—Mohammed Atta, Marwan al-Shehhi and Ziad Jarrah—Terry McDermott has made a start, gathering all the biographical information he could detect in Germany. McDermott wanted to know who the people were that committed such a monstrous deed. The answer he arrived at was for himself 'truly troubling': they were 'regrettably...fairly ordinary men'. He found they were young Muslims who lived mainly in the diaspora and who had turned into convicted believers without admitting the slightest doubt. 'It is this certainty, not the belief itself that causes the problem', he notes.[153] A similar study has been carried out by Stephen Holmes. His research likewise revolves around the predicament of young, educated Muslims in the German diaspora who felt alienated from their home society as well as from their host society and who cultivated their anger and frustration in small religious circles. Mohammed Atta, for example, felt personally hurt by the low esteem serious Muslim believers enjoy in today's Egypt.[154]

2. Ghazwa*s on Manhattan and Washington*

There is external evidence for the meaning the perpetrators attributed to the attack. Members of al-Qaeda called it 'the Manhattan *ghazwa*', 'the two *ghazwa*s from Washington and New York', or 'the Operation Holy Tuesday'.[155] The *Spiritual Manual* confirms the former understanding when it calls the attack a *ghazwa*, a raid (on the path of God) (1/3; 3/1). For a study of the meanings of *ghazwa*, the *Spiritual Manual* turns out to be a rich source. It enables us to grasp how the perpetrators, their accomplices and aids, and other Muslim sympathizers conceived of their attack and what meaning they attributed to it. In addition, it reveals where that meaning derived from.

In Islam, waging war for the sake of God has a long history and goes back to the very beginning of the religion. After his migration to Medina in AD 622 Muḥammad participated in at least 27 campaigns and delegated some 59 others—on average nine campaigns per year. The battles are divided into different groups: the five 'thematic' battles (Badr AD 624, Uhud 625, Khandaq 627, Mecca 630 and Hunayn 630), raids against the Bedouin, attacks against Jewish tribes and three raids against Byzantine and Syria. The historical evidence indicates the paramount importance of jihad to the early Muslim community.[156] Later, when officials of Islamic states announced a war against infidels and mobilized their armies, the individual Muslim believer was expected to serve in the armed forces. Yet there existed a stronger religious version of this duty. A Muslim could prove the sincerity of his faith by engaging voluntarily in struggles against the infidels, independent of any military necessity. Muḥammad's statement that every Prophet brings some kind of world-rejecting monasticism (*rahbāniyya*), and that the monasticism of his community consists in the jihad, testifies to a close link between a believer's rejection of the world and the war against infidels in Islam.[157] According to classical Islamic texts, the sincere Islamic fighter prepares for war by world denial, eulogising God, reciting from the Koran, performing prayers, saying *dhikr*, and fasting.[158] Albrecht Noth, who has studied in painstaking detail the relation between ascetic practices and war against the infidels in classical Arabic literature, draws the conclusion that 'in Islam the struggle against the infidels was regarded and proclaimed as a kind of worship'.[159]

The mere existence of such a belief in Islam cannot explain its present application. The sociological theory of social action emphasizes that there is no causal, necessary, or compelling relation between the beliefs people hold and the way they act. On the contrary! Any proper understanding of any social action has to acknowledge the absence of that link. According to social scientists, no actor converts a religious belief into practice independent of the situation in which he happens to be. The German social scientist Hartmut Esser reminds us of a concept formulated by William and Dorothy Thomas in 1928 and called the 'Thomas-Theorem': 'If men define situations as real, they are real in their consequences'.[160] For any definition of a situation, it is crucial that it is neither compelled by the external social reality nor by one's religious norms. The definition of a situation rests on the creativity of the actor, who selects the practical model for his/her acting out of a stock of transmitted doctrines, norms, values and paradigms and establishes by means of his/her choice the reason for his/her acting. Human action is not contingent on a situation, but 'the situation is *constitutive* of action'. How we define the situation is crucial to how we act (Hans Joas).[161] Although an actor remains dependent on external conditions and on transmitted beliefs, neither determines his/her definition of a situation. This approach affects our understanding of religion. Religion should not be regarded as an immutable heritage, but as a means of positioning oneself in a context —religion is not baggage, but a positioning system[162]

The lack of a direct link between belief and action challenges students of religions. It places a large question mark over the conventional wisdom that the violence of Muslims (or of Jews and Christians) has its roots in monotheism, or—more generally—that monotheism generates intolerance. The disadvantage of undermining that wisdom is compensated for by the chance to deal more adequately with a dilemma that also impedes the study of 9/11. Either the perpetrators of 9/11 were Muslims and therefore Islam has to be blamed for inspiring violence; or they were not Muslims and Islam is unable to contribute anything to our understanding of the attack. We move beyond that dilemma when we re-phrase our questions: Which norms and beliefs out of the stock of Islamic traditions has the *Spiritual Manual* selected in order to legitimate the attack? What is the rationale behind the selection in terms of the definition of the situation of Muslims in the present world? By tracing connections between the deed and the actors, and between the actors and the *Spiritual Manual* we may grasp how the perpetrators conceived of their deed and how they generated the meaning of their action.

3. *The Renewal of Intent*

The *Manual* divided the attack into three stages (*marḥala*): the night before, at the airport, and in the aircraft. The stages turn the practical steps of the planned attack into mental representations that can be reflected on and practiced for in advance. The *Manual* functions as technical instructions for the attack and as a spiritual preparation for a *ghazwa.* It opens with the words: 'Mutual pledge (*bay'a*) to die and renewal of intention' (1/1). The first part of the sentence refers to the social formation of the 19 attackers and will be dealt with in the next chapter. Here we focus on the second part that is crucial for reconstructing the actors' understanding of their deed. In Islamic law, 'intent' (*niyya*) is a fundamental category. 'An act of worship without *niyya* is invalid, and so is *niyya* without act'.[163] Sayyid Quṭb applied the principle to religious militancy. So did his brother Mohammed Quṭb, who taught at the University of Jidda and exerted some influence on one of his students there, Usama bin Ladin. The genuine faith of a Muslim has to be judged primarily in terms of internal intention (*niyya*), not of external action.[164] Likewise the *Spiritual Manual* justifies brute violence in light of the pure intention of the actor.[165]

But what does this mean in the case of a *ghazwa*? The *Spiritual Manual* itself provides an answer to that question when it praises Ali, cousin and son-in-law of the Prophet, as a model for how to fight:

> Do not take vengeance for yourself, but make your strike and everything else for the sake of God. Take for example 'Alī Ibn Abī Ṭālib. When he once fought against an unbeliever, the unbeliever spat on him. 'Alī then let his sword pause and did not strike him. Only afterwards did he strike him. (3/13) After the battle, one of the companions asked him why he had done so, why he had not struck the unbeliever, and first left off and only later struck him. 'Alī answered: 'When he spat on me, I feared I would strike him out of vengeance. Therefore I held my sword', or how he said. (3/14) When he had called the intention (*niyya*) to mind, he turned to him and struck and killed him. All this means that the human being should prepare his soul in a very short time, and then all he does is for the sake of God. (3/15)

The offence against Ali deserves vengeance, of course, and the choice of this case certainly reflects the mood of the young Muslims. The *Manual* acknowledges that mood but reminds them that it is the diligent preparation of the violent response that determines its nature: whether it is an act of personal revenge or a campaign in the name of God. This conception of violence explains why the *Manual* does not specify the alleged offences committed by the United States against Islam, put forward by Usama bin Ladin as reasons for his declarations of war against the United States in 1996 and 1998. Instead of mentioning any of his grievances, the actor must perform the deed in a way that speaks for itself. And it does! Targets of the attacks were today's citadels of paganism: the stock market of Wall Street represented by the World Trade Center; the military might at its home base in the Pentagon; and Capitol Hill, centre of the political power that the plane did not reach because it crashed prematurely in Pennsylvania.[166]

In *The Neglected Duty* we encounter a similar Islamic framing of bellicose violence, used to justify the assassination of the Egyptian president Anwar al-Sadat in 1981. According to the author of *The Neglected Duty*, Abd al-Salam Faraj (1954–1982), jihad has three aspects: struggle against one's own soul, against Satan, and against the infidels and hypocrites (§88). These three aspects are part and parcel of one and the same action and may not be separated into successive stages (§89). Abd al-Salam Faraj strongly rejects the distinction between a spiritual Great jihad waged only against one's soul and a military Small jihad against infidels, and regards the concept of a purely spiritual Great jihad as a fabricated tradition (§90). Jihad in its three aspects is an individual religious duty like praying and fasting. Therefore, a young man need not ask his parents for permission to participate (§87).[167] Faraj developed an understanding of a *ghazwa* as a spiritual and militant action that is similar to the tripartite division of the action in the *Manual*: the struggle with one's own soul during the night before, overcoming the fear of the Satanic power at the airport, and the fight against the infidels inside and outside the aircraft. In support of this claim that there is some influence from Faraj is the fact that excerpts of Faraj's writing were part of the training received by Muslim fighters in Afghan camps.[168] This training taught combatants that militant action needs to be performed as a spiritual path.

4. *The First Stage of the Night Before: Attaining a State of Purity*

The *Manual* admonishes the young Muslims to purify their bodies and their souls for the *ghazwa* during the night before their departure. Fifteen exercises of different kinds are prescribed, from a recapitulation of the plan to recitals, prayers, meditations, and purifications. Surahs 8 and 9 are chosen for memorisation. The Prophet himself, the writer of the *Manual* tells us, had ordered the surah to be recited before the raid against the unbelievers (*ghazwa*); rich booty was the reward. Applying the principle today assumes that contemporary Muslims are again in a situation like that of Medina and that they are threatened by the enemies of Islam.[169] Recitation, *dhikr*, implies a transformation of past histories into present reality; it makes the speaker share the miraculous powers of the Prophet. The selection of the two surahs is significant. Both surahs originated at a time when Muḥammad had left Mecca, had begun establishing an Islamic state in Medina, and then went to war against the Meccans. Muḥammad, the persecuted prophet, turned into Muḥammad, the statesman.[170] Whereas during his years in Mecca the Prophet practiced kindness and tact in propagating the message, now warfare for the sake of an Islamic polity became incumbent on the Prophet and his adherents. At the heart of the issue is the Sword Verse, surah 9:5:

> And when the sacred months are over, kill the polytheists wherever you find them, and take them captive, and besiege them, and lie in wait for them in every stratagem [of war]; but if they repent, establish regular prayers, and pay *zakāt* then open the way for them, for God is the dispenser of mercy.

The shift from tolerance to militancy is a critical issue in Islamic theology. Many Islamic scholars assume that the Sword Verse has replaced preceding revelations in accordance with Koran 2:106: 'Any sign (or verse) which We annul or consign to oblivion We replace with a better or a similar one'.[171] This understanding is shared by Abd al-Salam Faraj in his *Neglected Duty*. He cites scholars claiming that the words: 'Kill the polytheists wherever you find them' and 'Fighting is prescribed to you' (2:216) invalidated no less than 114 verses in 54 surahs that prescribed living in peace with the polytheists.[172] Other Muslim scholars have contradicted the concept of an abrogation of tolerant surahs. The Egyptian Mufti Sheikh Jadd al-Haqq, in his rejection of the *Neglected Duty*, did nothing more than point to the words that follow the pertinent sentence: 'If they [the polytheists] repent and establish regular prayer and pay zakāt, then open the way for them, for God is the dispenser of mercy'. And Abdullahi Ahmed An-Na'im rejects in principle the idea of an abrogation (*naskh*) of earlier revelations.[173]

In order to carry out the duty of jihad, the manual recommends practices of self-conditioning that resemble spiritual techniques among Sufis and Muslim Brothers:[174]

> Reminding yourself of unconditional obedience that night, as you will encounter decisive situations that require 100 per cent unconditional obedience. Pull yourself together, make yourself understand, convince yourself and incite yourself to this action. (1/4)

'The carnal self is the enemy of the vow to die, selfishly seeking to hang on to life' is Cole's comment on this admonition. The young man should pray in the middle of the night to facilitate matters and to avoid detection (1/5), recite the Koran (1/6) and purify his heart:

> Purify your heart, cleanse it from stains and forget or ignore that thing named 'World'. The time of playing is over, and the true appointment has come. How much of our lifetime did we waste! Why don't we use these hours profitably by offering acts pleasing to God and pious deeds?! (1/7)

The instructions employ a language of world denial. World denial becomes a means of salvation (1/8). If the warrior faces difficulties, they are God's trial in order to raise his status (1/9); he can put all his trust in God. With God's permission, even a tiny group can defeat a large one (1/10). After more prayers (1/11) some religious advice is given, including that one should spit on oneself and one's belongings while the Koran is recited, and the need for the gruesome sharpening of the sacrificial knife and the proper arrangement of one's clothing (1/12-14). The morning prayer with the entire group (*jamā'a*) and a ritual ablution mark the end of the first stage. The Muslim actor has attained a state of ritual purity (1/15).

5. *The Second Stage at the Airport: Overcoming the Fear of the Satanic Power of Western Civilization*

The second stage anticipates the situation at the airport. The main issue of this stage is the protection the believer needs in a world ruled by Satanic powers. Here the *Manual* knows an effective means:

> Wherever you go and whatever you do, always perform the prayers. God grants his pious servants protection, facilitation, success, strengthening, assistance and everything else. (2/15)

The warrior can remain calm; the angels will protect him even if he does not notice it. Crucial for tackling the situation in the airport is the instruction to recite the supplication, 'God is greater than all his creation' (2/3) and to ask God that the enemies will be unable to recognize him so that he remains undetected (2/3). 'Their equipment, their gates and their technology, all of this does neither benefit nor harm, except with God's permission' (2/6). Only the followers of Satan are afraid of that technology:

'Fear is a great act of worship which is permitted to be offered only to God, and he is most worthy of it' (2/7):

> Those who are enchanted by Western civilization are people who have drunk their love and reverence with cold water. They feared their (own) weak, fragile equipment. 'Therefore do not fear them; but fear you Me, if you are believers'. [Surah 3:175]. Fear is a great act of worship. The followers of God and the believers offer it only to the one and only God in whose hand are all things. Be sure that God will frustrate the guile of the unbelievers as he has said, 'That for you; and that God weakens the unbelievers' guile'. [Surah 8:18] (2/8)

While the friends of Satan are impressed by 'Western civilization', the true believer fears God alone. Unnoticed by others, the believer is reciting 'There is no God except Allah' (*lā ilāha illā llāh*) (2/10). The Prophet himself has revealed the power of these words: 'Whoever says: 'There is no God but God' in full belief will enter paradise... If the seven heavens and the seven earths were put in one scale-pan, and *lā ilāha illā llāh* in the other one, the latter would outweigh the first' (2/10).

The *Manual* locates the enemy as only here, nowhere else: It is 'Western civilization' and the fear and fascination it incites in people. It is not impossible that the *Manual* here refers to Samuel Huntington's thesis of an irreconcilable conflict between Christian and Muslim culture.[175] A particular diagnosis of the present age underlies the reflection on fear, as David Cook has argued. In the present age, in which Islam is threatened with destruction and in which weakness is placed in the hearts of the Muslims, Muslims arise and demonstrate that fear can be replaced by the fearlessness of the true believer.[176] Connected with this construction of the superiority of the Muslim warrior is the notion of his concealment. The soldier of the ultimate power remains unrecognized in the realm of Satanic powers. In a world filled with lies, the true believer has to deceive the unbelievers as to his true identity. Protection is achieved by the practice of dissimulation. But concealment is not his own achievement. The believer must pray for it (1/5); it is God who makes it effective. Only He knows his servant; the success of his concealment is proof of his being elected. The principle of dissimulation has a long prehistory and was already practiced by the ancient Gnostics, who regarded the material world as created by a Satanic power which made it unable to recognize the servants of the hidden God. Concealing their identity was part of their faith. This principle was later adopted and revised by Muslims.[177]

The notion of the hidden believer touches a basic idea of Jihad-Islam, expressed most clearly by Sayyid Quṭb. The external world is so deeply corrupted by the power of paganism and disbelief that truth has been forced to retreat into the hearts and minds of the individuals. The precedence of an interior faith over external actions explains why some of the attackers could live a Western lifestyle, shave their beards and drink alcohol.[178] The relationship between the external visible world and the internal invisible faith has been broken.

6. *The Third Stage in the Aircraft: Attacking the Infidels and the Gift of Martyrdom*

Finally, the third stage on the path of God is the attack. Unnoticed, the hero has entered the plane, tacitly reciting prayers and parts of the Koran. Now the issue of martyrdom becomes central. 'And ask God to grant you martyrdom while you are moving forward and not retreating, persevering and hoping for God's reward' (3/7). Martyrdom is not an achievement by the believer, but is granted by God alone.[179] The readiness to sacrifice one's life is necessary; but God's granting of the prayer is decisive:

> In close combat, strike firmly like heroes who do not wish to return to this world. Exclaim loudly *Allāhu akbar*, because the exclaiming of *Allāhu akbar* instils fright into the unbelievers' hearts. And the Most High has said, 'So smite above the necks, and smite every finger of them!' [Surah 8:12] (3/9)

The attack is conceived in terms of the militant Medina scenario of surah 8. The re-enactment of that *ghazwa* ensures the warrior a superior reward: a wedding with the heavenly brides:

> And know that the Gardens have adorned themselves with their most distinct garbs and the paradise virgins are calling you, saying, 'O friend of God, come', wearing their nicest clothing. (3/10)

The topic of the wedding of the martyr with the heavenly brides is to Western observers particularly strange. Malise Ruthven has tried to open a path towards our understanding of this theme. Ruthven reminds us that Al-Ghazali (d. AD 1111) saw the sexual imagery of paradise as an inducement to righteousness. The state of spiritual fulfilment can only be described in terms of familiar experiences.[180]

The violence in the plane is conceived of as a re-enactment of the Medina *ghazwa*s, in particular the War of the Trench. According to Ibn Isḥāq, in AD 627 a coalition consisting of Jews, the pagan Arab tribe called the Quraysh, and Muslim 'hypocrites' was defeated by the Prophet who had defended Medina by digging a fortified ditch. The writer of the *Manual* picks up the pertinent notion of 'Confederates' (*al-aḥzāb*), a coalition of the different kinds of enemies of Muḥammad. When asking God for victory, he recalls their defeat:

> And God's Prophet said, 'O God, who you have sent down the Book, moved the clouds and defeated the factions, defeat them and make us victorious. O God, defeat them and make them tremble. (3/6)

The composer of the *Manual* defines the source of the present threat to Islam as an alliance between rulers who are only nominally Muslim and external enemies of Islam.[181]

The attackers should be happy to perform the duty of the raid; killing is a sacrifice, offered for the sake of their parents (3/11). In accordance with the custom of the Prophet, some form of symbolic booty should be taken from the killed, for example, a cup or a glass of water, if possible (3/11 and 3/20). The custom of the (*sunna*) of the Prophet prescribes the capture and killing of the prisoners (3/16). When all goes as planned, the brothers from the apartment are to congratulate each other (3/17).

When the end draws close, the *Manual* recommends reciting some Koranic or poetic verses concerning the eternal life of martyrs (3/18-19).

> When the true promise and the zero hour approach, tear your suit and open your chest welcoming death on the path of God. Always mind God, either by ending with the ritual prayer (*ṣalāt*), if this is possible, starting it seconds before the target, or let your last words be, 'There is no God but God, and Muḥammad is his Prophet'. After that, God willing, the meeting in the highest paradise will follow through God's mercy. (3/21-23)

The last moment of life is decisive. All sins committed before it are swept away by an act like martyrdom. As David Cook suggests: 'One's final actions are the key to the judgement accorded to a person's entire life'.[182]

The *Manual* thus frames the attack in terms of early Islamic battles—including actions like looting or killing captives that seem out of place in a hijacked plane destined to crash into a building. Apparently the success of the attack depends on correctly and punctiliously re-enacting the *ghazwa* of the Prophet.

7. *The Subjective Meaning of the Attack: Enforcing the Fear of God*

The meaning attributed to the violence in the *Manual* has precursors in Lebanon during the 1980s. The United States and France left Lebanon after terrifying suicide attacks were carried out on the barracks of their troops in October 1983. Some years later Israel followed. The withdrawal of these powers contributed tremendously to the high esteem suicide attacks enjoy in the Middle East. No one ever imagined or could imagine that a few dedicated Muslims could drive out from Lebanon the technologically superior American, French and Israeli troops. Yet they did. This success had an impact on Islamic theology. The leader of the Shi'i community in Lebanon, Ayatollah Fadlallah, praised the actions against military targets as a 'rebellion against fear'. Martin Kramer summarizes Fadlallah's ideas as follows:

> The great [Western] powers inspire 'alarm and fear' among the oppressed, who have no more than 'children's toys' to mount their opposition. But by conquering their fear, through acceptance of the virtue of martyrdom, the oppressed can evoke alarm and fear among the oppressors. America and West, recalls one Hezbollah leader [i.e. Sadiq al-Musawi], 'hurriedly ran away from three Muslims who loved martyrdom' and sacrificed themselves in suicidal attacks.[183]

The global arrogance of the West represents a global unbelief, Fadlallah argued in an interview.[184] The power of the faithful consists in the ability to overcome the natural fear of death and to make arrogant Western civilisation tremble. The battle-cry *Allāhu akbar* that resounded also in the hijacked aircrafts expresses that aspiration.[185] Just as the Prophet, with only a few followers, defeated superior pagan armies, so the faithful Muslim today is able to humiliate Western civilization by means of its own panic. Usama bin Ladin's declaration of war in 1996 opened with three quotations from the Koran, placing the fear of God (*taqwā*) at the centre of the faith.[186] By inciting fear in the adherents of Western civilization, the warrior gives practical proof of the existence of a power infinitely mightier than Western civilization. The traditional notion of God's absolute power no longer has a metaphysical foundation alone, but is also apparent in the practice of the believers.

Conclusions

The *Spiritual Manual* allows us to retrieve the *subjective meaning* that the perpetrators and their sympathizers attributed to the attacks. They understood the attack in terms of a *ghazwa* that occurred at the time of the formation of an Islamic state, in particular the War of the Trench in AD 627. Similar to Sayyid Quṭb, they conceived of the contemporary situation in terms of the beginning of Islam. The Prophet first established the true religion in Mecca in the hearts of men, before he established it by force in the form of a state with public laws in Medina.[187] Since the world was (and today again is) dominated by pagan forces, only secretly and gradually can an autonomous community of believers arise and challenge its Satanic power.

The believers attacking these forces need to answer specific requirements, if they wish to walk on the path of God and turn their attack into a sacred deed. The requirements are:

1. a pure intention, not tainted by personal feelings of vengeance;
2. an understanding that they re-enact Muḥammad's raids;
3. a fear of God, displayed as a readiness for self-martyrdom and for instilling terror in the heart of unbelievers.

The fighters were convinced that God would assist them when attacking the headquarters of contemporary paganism. The *Spiritual Manual* does not explicitly refer to any of the injuries Muslims are suffering—allegedly or actually—at the hands of the United States. Vindication of the attack is sought elsewhere, as the example of Ali demonstrates. As another *Spiritual Manual* for the jihad told its readers: 'What matters is not the act, but the intention (*niyya*) of the martyr'.[188] As the model of a person who prepares for a *ghazwa*, Ali transformed a desire for vengeance into an unemotional act of divine punishment. Purity of intention is crucial for violence to be exercised correctly.

7

The Social Matrix of the Attack

Hans G. Kippenberg

1. *A Mutual Pledge to Die and the Hamburg Cell*

The *Manual* in the hands of the attacking groups enables us to reconstruct how the operation socially was organized. It opens with the words: 'Mutual pledge (*bay'a*) to die and renewal of intent'. In the history of Islam, *bay'a* signifies a solemn act by which faithful Muslims declare their allegiance towards a charismatic leader and by which they establish relations of brotherliness among them.[189] Sufi associations of young men, the *futuwwa*, were established according to that principle.[190] The modern Egyptian Muslim Brothers adopted the principle. The Muslim Brotherhood consisted of laymen dedicated to establishing Islamic values in their personal and social life; it admitted new members by an 'oath of brotherhood' (*bay'at al-ukhuwwa*).[191] The practice spread among militant groups at the fringe of the group. Mohammed Abd al-Salam Faraj (1954–1982), author of *The Neglected Duty*, the book which formulated the creed of the assassins of President Sadat (1981), raised the question whether an 'oath of allegiance to fight until death' was restricted to the Prophet alone or could also be sworn to other commanders. Faraj argued that it could; an oath of allegiance till death is permissible (§§95-97).[192] Our *Manual* likewise presumes that the participants of the 9/11 operation had pledged allegiance to Usama bin Ladin till death.

The nineteen attackers belonged to different groups, organizations, and nations. Their cooperation was coordinated by Bin Ladin and his aids. The Hamburg cell provided three of the four pilots and the coordinator of the attacks; a fourth pilot was added by Bin Ladin in Afghanistan; two men close to Bin Ladin joined the teams; the rest were Muslim fighters (Jihadists) from Saudi Arabia, charged with hijacking and controlling the aircrafts.

The Islamists from Harburg, a district of Hamburg, stayed in a private apartment on Marienstrasse 54, run by a group called *dār al-anṣār* ('The House of the Helpers'). Mohammed Atta, Ramzi Binalshib, and Marwan al-Shehhi saw themselves living in a time similar to that of Medina, when the Prophet was in urgent need of people to help him gain recognition and power for the new community. Young Muslims moved into the Marienstrasse community, while others left it. In the course of two years, more than a dozen men registered under this address with the local authorities, as Terry McDermott disclosed when researching the Hamburg cell.[193] The men became acquainted in the al-Kuds Mosque in the centre of Hamburg, where Arab Muslims joined together to perform their prayers, listen to sermons, and attend or organize classes in Islam. In 1997, Ziad Jarrah joined the group without moving into the apartment.

The duty of jihad was a major issue in the conversations among the young 'helpers'.[194] A veteran of the war in Afghanistan and a German citizen originally from Syria, Muhammad Haydar Zammar, preached in his sermons in the al-Kuds Mosque that jihad is a duty, neglected by most Muslims. He encouraged his audience to actually perform the jihad. The 'Helpers' from the Marienstrasse considered Chechnya a proper place for their commitment. According to the *9/11 Commission Report*, Zammar was a 'possible recruiter of Hamburg cell members'. But his impact on the group was probably more in the field of belief and persuasion than of organizing contacts.[195] A crucial role in actually recruiting the students for the brotherhood of Bin Ladin was performed by Abu Musab, whose real name was Mohamedou Ould Slahi. He was an al-Qaeda operative, staying in Duisburg. By chance, Ramzi Binalshib came across his name and visited him along with Ziad Jarrah and Marwan al-Shehhi. Slahi told them that it was impossible to get to Chechnya directly; he recommended Afghanistan instead, where they could train for jihad before travelling onward to Chechnya. After obtaining Pakistani visas, they should return for further instructions on how to reach Afghanistan.[196]

In fall 1999 their plans were realised. Together with Mohammed Atta they travelled from Hamburg to Pakistan, each following a separate route in order to avoid attention. From Quetta in Pakistan they travelled by car to an Afghan training camp near Kandahar, where they were introduced to Bin Ladin. When they arrived, a new international league of Muslims fighting against the enemies of Islam was about to evolve. Its leader was Usama bin Ladin, and his base was called al-Qaeda.

2. *Usama bin Ladin's Declarations of War (1996 and 1998) and the Egyptian Jihad*

Al-Qaeda had its origins in the war against the Soviet Union in Afghanistan (1979–1989). When the war drew to an end, Bin Ladin along with his seniors created a register of the Muslim fighters who had participated in that successful struggle. The volunteers about to return to their home countries were regarded as potential fighters for future militant conflicts with the enemies of Islam. After the retreat of the Red Army from Afghanistan, Bin Ladin was forced to go to Sudan with his family and a small group of adherents. Years later, in 1996, when the Taliban seized power, he moved to Afghanistan along with his still small group of adherents. In Afghanistan, his 'register' (the database containing the names of Jihadists) began to develop a social life of its own. Members of the Egyptian Jihād, lead by the physician Ayman al-Ẓawāhirī (b. 1953),[197] left Egypt and merged with Bin Ladin's group in 1998.[198] The Egyptian doctrine of jihad, along with the oil wealth of Saudi Arabia and the religious motivation of the rank and file of Islamists of Saudi Arabia, established a powerful new organisation.[199]

In the year of his move to Afghanistan, Bin Ladin published an epistle to the Muslim brothers across the world.[200] He summoned them to join their Arab brothers in the war against the Judeo-Christian alliance and its supporters. The blood of the brothers has been spilled, their property looted in Palestine, Iraq, and Lebanon, Bin Ladin claimed. Bin Ladin mentions a further eleven countries by name, in which Muslims had become victims of massacres. The latest and most serious attack and the greatest disaster that ever befell Muslims in their history, in Bin Ladin's view, was the occupation of Saudi Arabia by US troops. The cornerstone of the Islamic world, the country of the two holy places, and the place of revelation, had been desecrated. The regime of the Saudis tolerated the occupation and lost its legitimacy:

> I say to our Muslim brothers across the world: your brothers in Palestine and in the land of the Two Holy Places are calling upon your help and asking you to take part in fighting against the enemy, your enemies, the Israelis and the Americans.

The place where this epistle was proclaimed is called Khorasan—a religious designation in early Islamic history for parts of today's Afghanistan, from where the Muslim Messias, the Mahdī, was expected to rise and liberate the Muslim countries from the enemies of God.

Two years later, in February 1998, a new declaration in the name of the 'World Islamic Front' was issued. In addition to Bin Ladin's name, it was signed by Ayman al-Ẓawāhirī as Emir of the Jihad Group in Egypt and three representatives of other Islamist groups in Egypt, Pakistan, and Bangladesh, one of them Rifa'i Ahmad Taha for the Egyptian al-Jamā'a al-Islāmiyya.[201] The new declaration is shorter than that of 1996. It opens with a recital from Koran 9:5. It calls on the faithful to kill the polytheists wherever they are found. Never before has the Arabian Peninsula suffered such a calamity as today, the declaration stated; Crusader hordes are spreading like locusts and consuming all its wealth; nations are joining their forces against the Muslims as if fighting over a bowl of food —an event of eschatological significance.[202] The declaration went on to claim that a huge conspiracy against Islam was taking place. America had occupied the holiest parts of the Islamic lands. Despite the great devastation that America had already inflicted upon the Iraqi people, it was trying to repeat its horrific massacres; the wars America wages for its religious and economic purposes serve the interest of the petty Jewish state and aim at fragmenting all states in the region, turning them into paper mini-states. All these American crimes and sins are a proclamation of war against God, his Messenger, and his people. The signatories then in common pronounce their judgment (*ḥukm*):

> To kill the Americans and their allies—civilians and military—is an individual duty incumbent upon every Muslim in any country, in order to liberate the al-Aqsa Mosque [= Palestine] and the Holy Mosque [= Saudi Arabia] from their grip, so that their armies leave all the territory of Islam, defeated, broken, and unable to threaten any Muslim... We also call on the religious scholars, their leaders, their youth, and their soldiers, to launch the raid on the soldiers of Satan, the Americans.[203]

These words already envision a 'raid' on the soldiers of the 'Satanic' power. The manner in which this attack is recommended betrays ideas from Ayman al-Ẓawāhirī and the Egyptian Jihād.

> Believers, why, when it is said to you, 'Go and fight in God's way', do you dig your heels into the earth?[204] Do you prefer this world to the life to come? How small is the enjoyment of this world, compared with the life to come!

The *Manual* teaches a similar world denial. Performing the raid on Manhattan and Washington is a spiritual act. Though the crimes and sins of America are in the sphere of foreign policy, they are regarded as offences against God, his Prophet, and his people. This understanding affects the status of those who fight against this enemy; it renders the raid a means of achieving personal salvation. Jihad is not restricted to the defence of a particular territory; it is part of a war against the global enemies of God and is based on an Islamic ethics of conviction. The new martyrs, as Farhad Khosrokhavar called these fighters, do not die in the context of a defence of a national community or territory; martyrdom is seen as self-sacrifice in the service of the confession of faith, of *shahāda*.[205] A Muslim who decides to die in attacking the global enemy of God, independent of any territory, belongs to a global *umma*.

The first attacks that resulted from that declaration happened—not by chance—outside Islamic countries. The targets were two US embassies in East Africa, in front of which on 7 August 1998 car bombs were detonated, killing and injuring many people and causing enormous damage.

3. *Al-Qaeda: Network and Hierarchy*

The Arabic designation *al-qā'ida* means a base, a camp, a home, or a foundation. It indicates a purpose or a function, not an existing group.[206] Bin Ladin accepted the latter meaning not without hesitation, when he was interrogated by others who used it as a designation for a group.[207] He and his followers referred to themselves differently, as 'The International Front for the jihad against Jews and Crusaders' or 'The Islamic Army for the Liberation of the Holy Places'. Scholars have suggested for al-Qaeda the definition 'militant Islamists with a connection to Afghanistan' or 'transnational militant Islamism'.[208] The designation 'Bin-Ladin-Brotherhood' has also been proposed;[209] it seems particularly appropriate.[210] The vacillation among terms mirrors the fluid character of the social entity. When the trails of the bombing campaign against the American Embassies in East Africa in 1998 led to Bin Ladin, President Clinton referred to the enemy as 'Bin Ladin's network'. Jason Burke, in scrutinizing the report of an FBI interrogation of a suspect, points out that the suspect conceived of al-Qaeda as a network, while the FBI searched for information about a coherent, structured organization.[211]

Within the al-Qaeda network we must recognise different layers of belonging.[212] Besides the inner circle of Bin Ladin and his confidantes, a second circle existed of those who pledged allegiance to Bin Ladin.[213] Recently discovered sources give further details. A *Tārīkh Usāma* ('Usama's History'), recovered from the hard drive of the computer of a Muslim charity in Bosnia in 2002, contains a substantial number of electronic files and documents that detail the rise of al-Qaeda in 1988. The minutes of a crucial three-day meeting in August 1988 are filed beside a list of requirements specifying the wording of the oath of allegiance for new members:

> The pledge [to join al-Qaeda]. The pledge of God and his covenant is upon me, to listen and obey the superiors, who are doing this work, in energy, early-rising, difficulty, and easiness, and for his superiority upon us, so that the word of God will be the highest, and His religion victorious.[214]

After the retreat of the Red Army the members had to swear the oath of allegiance (*bay'a*) to the Emir Bin Ladin.[215] Not more than 20 to 30 per cent of the trainees were offered the opportunity to join by oath.[216]

This brotherhood was open for new faithful followers from other countries. A study by Marc Sageman of the biography of 172 members of al-Qaeda reveals that social bonds prior to the affiliation—friendship, kinship, discipleship, worship—were crucial for joining the network:[217]

> The process of joining the jihad was more a bottom-up than a top-down activity. A lot of Muslim young men want to join the jihad but do not know how. Joining the jihad is more akin to the process of applying to a highly selective college. Many try to get in but only a few succeed... I did not detect any active top-down organizational push to increase al Qaeda's membership. The pressure came from the bottom up.[218]

Despite Sageman's observations, there is also some evidence for recruitment from above. Roland Jacquard has assembled information on deliberate recruitment by Bin Ladin confidantes in North Africa and Europe.[219] There is much to support the thesis of Renate Mayntz, that al-Qaeda combines two elements: hierarchical organization and vertical network. Such a hybrid form displays certain characteristics: the lowest units are both autonomous as well as subject to central control; they are isolated from each other, but nevertheless indirectly connected; the activities of the members are inspired by their commitment to a guiding master idea.[220] These characteristics certainly apply to the attack of 9/11. Even with such a correction, Marc Sageman is right in pointing out that informal, weak ties among like-minded friends, family, and so on constitute a particular strength of the social movement of global jihad.[221] The coordination of actions that derive from a commitment by all participants to a common mission is more successful than one based on hierarchy alone.[222] But without some kind of hierarchy, there is no cooperation of the diverse social units.

The relationship between the two principles of (vertical) hierarchy and (horizontal) network had already been spelled out by Ibn Khaldun in the fifteenth century. Ibn Khaldun wanted to explain why religious leaders in North Africa were able to mobilize the fragmented and rival social units again and again, uniting them in an encompassing social movement, which resulted in a new dynasty. A heterogeneous following could be successfully unified only by a superior authority—the transcending prestige of a religious leader. The common denominator was *'aṣabiyya*: a solidarity and loyalty that arose from kinship loyalties extended to other social units, and which could generate the formation of a state.[223]

Among the diverse social units cooperating with al-Qaeda were groups that operated independently in foreign countries. Sometimes their cooperation was restricted to no more than one issue or action; sometimes it concerned only subgroups. Jason Burke compared these mutual relationships with the anti-globalisation movement and called it 'a loose "network of networks"'.[224] Since Bin Ladin possessed extraordinary financial means, the cooperation sometimes resembled an international enterprise that assigned some of its tasks to local entrepreneurs.[225] Bin Ladin's substantial financial means did not derive from his personal fortune alone, which is often overrated, but mostly from private Islamic charities under his control.[226]

4. *Social Bonds between the Attackers*

When members from the Hamburg cell arrived in Kandahar in 1999, Bin Ladin, along with his confidantes, was just beginning to consider an attack on the USA using aeroplanes. The first participants in the future operation were already selected, among them Khalid al-Mihdhar and Nawaf al-Hazmi from Saudi Arabia, both experienced fighters; they entered the United States via California in January 2000.[227] The new arrivals from Hamburg fitted the plan perfectly, since the students were technically skilled and spoke English fluently. Apparently, it was as a result of mutual interest that they were integrated into the 'Planes' Operation' after solemnly pledging their allegiance to Usama bin Ladin.[228] Mohammed Atta was appointed as Emir of the group. The four men were instructed to return to Germany and to enrol in flight-training—which they did first in Germany, and later in the United States.[229] After Ramzi Binalshibh's application for a visa was denied, he acted as a coordinator between the Hamburg cell and the military commander of al-Qaeda, Khalid Sheikh Mohammed, and his deputy Mohammed Atef.[230] In his function as pilot he was replaced by Hani Hanjour, who joined the Californian detachment.[231] During the summer of 2000, Bin Ladin and his aids selected thirteen more operatives, all from Saudi Arabia, except one from the United Arab Emirates. They were called the 'muscles', since their task was to hijack and control the planes. Only three of the hijackers had no ties with other participants. Some were brothers; four shared the same tribal affiliation; five came from the province of Asir that borders Yemen and which, due to its poverty, feeds resentment against the rule of the wealthy Saudi kings. Among these five was Abdulaziz al-Omari, the probable author of the *Spiritual Manual*.[232]

Since the *Manual* indicated 'airport' and 'plane' by abbreviations, one may wonder whether in fact all the young men knew the details of the plan in advance. In an interview Bin Ladin supported that doubt:

> The brothers who conducted the operation, all they knew was that they have a martyrdom operation and we asked each of them to go to America but they didn't know anything about the operation, not even one letter. But they were trained and we did not reveal the operation to them until they are [*sic*] there and just before they boarded the planes.[233]

Only the pilots were fully informed. The other combatants knew only that they were embarking on a suicide mission.

In place of—or in addition to—their civil name, all the hijackers adopted a new personal name, a *kunya*, as Yosri Fouda reports. A few weeks after his interview in Karachi, Ramzi Binalshibh sent Fouda a floppy disk answering some further questions. One of these was the exact *kunya* for each of the nineteen hijackers. In traditional Islamic culture a man or woman could adopt a new or additional name in the course of his or her life; a personal *kunya* indicates the bearer to be, for example, the father or mother of a son. This name was originally connected with the first son, but since early Islamic times it had lost these kinship roots and turned into a general marker of esteem.[234] That holds true in this case too. For example, Mohammed Atta was called Abu Abdu'l Rahman al-Masri. Literally this means 'father of the servant of the Beneficent, the Egyptian'. One of the most famous Abu Abdu'l Rahmans in Islamic history was somebody who donated much of his wealth to the Muslim army and to whom the Prophet gave the glad tidings that he would go to Paradise. Most of the fighters of 9/11 were named after similar Islamic figures: exemplary fighters or steadfast believers.[235] Since some of the names are not well known, one can suppose that the names were chosen by the fighters themselves. At what point this happened in the process of joining the network, the source does not betray—perhaps after the solemn oath of loyalty to Bin Ladin or after the young man had committed himself on video to die as martyr. In the latter case the name was given to a 'living martyr'.[236]

5. *The De-centralized Structure of Muslim Militants: Families (*usar*) and Clan (*'ashīra*)*

The attacks of 11 September 2001 were committed by Muslims who regarded themselves as a community engaged in the struggle for an Islamic state. In terms of their social relations, a closer look at Lebanon in the 1980s is illuminating. The group that took responsibility for the attacks on the barracks of US and French troops in Beirut in October 1983 called itself 'Islamic Jihad' (*al-jihād al-islamī*) and was linked to the Shi'i 'Party of God', the Hizbullah. Hizbullah was a network of *ulama* along with their students, held together by various religious, local, kindred, or political bonds and loyalties.[237] The leaders of that association denied any direct involvement in the attacks and contended that *Islamic Jihad* was not the name of an organization, but a designation for militant Muslims. The militant cells probably operated independently of each other, only loosely connected by somebody in the background, similar to a 'bunch of grapes'[238] or a 'telephone organization'.[239]

The decentralized structure of Islamic groups derived from the Muslim Brothers. In Egypt in 1943, in a period of increasing pressure by government and police, the Muslim Brothers established a flexible form of organization, which provided the chief instrument for mobilizing and for safeguarding the loyalty of its members. The 'family' (*usra*) became the basic unit of the Brothers; in Egypt an *usra* consisted of five members, one of them their head. Four of these 'families' (*usar*) formed a 'clan' (*'ashīra*), directed by the head of one of the 'families'.[240] This system spread to the Muslim Brothers in Jordan, Gaza, and Syria, where a 'family' could number up to ten members.[241]

This decentralized structure was more than simply a means of defending the organization in times of persecution. The founder of the Muslim Brothers, Hasan al-Banna (1906–1949), expected that the new social units would lead to a 'recovery of the Islamic person'; the members should become familiar with each other and take mutual responsibility. To this end they should meet at least once a week, perform common religious duties, engage in establishing Islam in the personal sphere, have meals together, attend the Friday prayers, and contribute financially to a common till. The 'family' was regarded as part of an Islamic cultural enclave in a world ruled by non-Islamic values and norms.[242]

This social form became particularly dominant among Muslims who understood the present age as a new period of ignorance and paganism (*jāhiliyya*). A major proponent of this diagnosis was the previously mentioned Sayyid Quṭb. The process through which the power of *jāhiliyya* can be driven back and an Islamic polity established was dependent on the strength of dedicated communities. A restoration of Islam in the public sphere required a revolution, led by a vanguard that starts by purging its consciousness of the impure power. When three faithful Muslims had been awoken by the faith, they could form a society (*jamā'a*) of their own, separating themselves from pagan society, and they could then become the spearhead of a movement (*ḥaraka*) struggling against it. This Islamization from below, as Kepel has called the model, was not unique to the Muslim Brothers, but was likewise propagated in the Islamic World by the Society for the Propagation of Islam, *Jamāʻat al-tablīgh*, founded in India in 1927. In a world and age in which a new paganism (*jāhiliyya*) ruled the former Islamic World, the faithful could preserve their faith only by establishing a community (*jamāʻa*). The social form of 'families' and 'clans' was an integral part of a scenario by which Islam could be established as a moral and legal order.[243]

6. *World Rejection as Cultural Milieu*

Max Weber, who studied religious 'world denial' much more intensively than anybody else, recognized that other-worldly values are by no means exclusively values of the beyond. 'Psychologically considered, man in quest of salvation has been primarily preoccupied by attitudes of the here and now', Weber pointed out.[244] The world renouncer experiences his opposition to the world not as a flight from the world, but as a victory over the temptations of this world: 'The ascetic who rejects the world sustains at least the negative inner relationship with it which is presupposed in the struggle against it'.[245] This is why Weber differentiates world-flight from world-rejection. Our study of the attacks of 11 September supports his point of view. The means to achieve salvation by *ghazwa* became a religious value of its own and generated new and other forms of religious expressions. The Jihadist songs performed by members of the Hamburg cell during a wedding and presented by Tilman Seidensticker in the next chapter, are an excellent example of this phenomenon. The practice of world rejection also was a driving force behind the *Spiritual Manual.*

The attackers' motivation must be separated from the meaning of their action, as I argued on pp. 47–48. The meaning of an action does not adequately explain why people perform it; the question of the motivation of the actors has to be addressed separately. The case of the Hamburg cell requires that the situation of young Muslims in the diaspora be included in the study. In this regard, Olivier Roy has proposed a fresh perspective. Islamism, fighting in the Middle East in vain for an Islamic state, is turning into personal religiosity. While Islamism failed politically, a neo-fundamentalism is flourishing as an Islamic principle by which to conduct one's life, similar to the lifestyle Max Weber depicted for the Christian Puritans. In the words of Oliver Roy: 'Post-Islamism means the privatisation of re-Islamisation'.[246] Young Muslims in the diaspora, despising their compatriots in the homelands as hypocrites, make Islam an ethical principle of their activities, undisturbed by state repression.

The shift from a social and political conception of Islam to an ethical one that resulted from that political failure has tremendous effects: it disconnects Islam from its territories and jihad from the defence of these territories. De-territorialization stimulates the spread of new forms of religiosity.[247] Objective religion embodied in an institution turns into a subjective personal religiosity. The *umma* looses its geographical dimension and becomes a global religious community, based on ethics. This appropriation of a Western type of religiosity does not diminish the tensions between Muslims and Western culture. On the contrary! When the confrontation between Islam and the West is cast in Western categories, the territorial borders may fade away, but the mental borders are all the more endorsed and defended.[248] As Terry McDermott has argued, the people who committed the deed of 9/11 were fairly ordinary men.[249] A similar finding has been reached by Stephen Holmes. His explanation of the rise of the Hamburg cell revolves around the predicament of young, educated Muslims in the German diaspora who felt alienated from their home society as well as from their host society and cultivated their anger and frustration in small religious circles.[250] This approach may explain, at least in part, why young Muslims decided to join al-Qaeda.

8

Jihad Hymns (*Nashīds*) as a Means of Self-motivation in the Hamburg Group

Tilman Seidensticker

1. *Bahaji's Wedding*

The unexpectedly significant role of ritual elements in the *Spiritual Manual* has a parallel in another first-hand source that sheds light on the 9/11 attackers' milieu. Among the body of evidence seized in connection with the Hamburg group, there is a videotape showing the wedding ceremony of Said Bahaji. Bahaji, born in Germany to a German mother and a Moroccan father and belonging to the Hamburg group, fled a few days before 9/11. He seems to be alive, as he still sends e-mails to his wife, who is of Turkish origin. The video was recorded on 9 October 1999, and it contains about 50 minutes of footage from the public wedding ceremony held in the al-Kuds Mosque in Hamburg. As is common in very strict Islamic circles, there were two separate gatherings: one for the female guests and one for the males. The video shows the men's gathering; among the 50 to 60 people attending, there were some children as well.[251] Among the guests were Ziad Jarrah and Marwan al-Shehhi, who lost their lives in the attacks of September 2001, and Ramzi Binalshibh. Binalshibh is one of the two chief planners of 9/11, the other one being Khalid Sheikh Mohammed; both have since been arrested in Pakistan and are presently in US detention at an unknown location.

Some parts of the ceremony conform to what one would expect to happen at a Muslim wedding. At the beginning, a young man of Turkish origin welcomes the guests in German, Arabic and Turkish and, among other things, expresses his delight at this Arabic–Turkish marriage, something that, he says, has regrettably gone out of fashion in the past 50 to 70 years. Later on, Bahaji thanks his guests for having accepted the invitation, adding that the Prophet Muḥammad imposed acceptance of such invitations as a religious duty on every Muslim. Shortly afterwards,

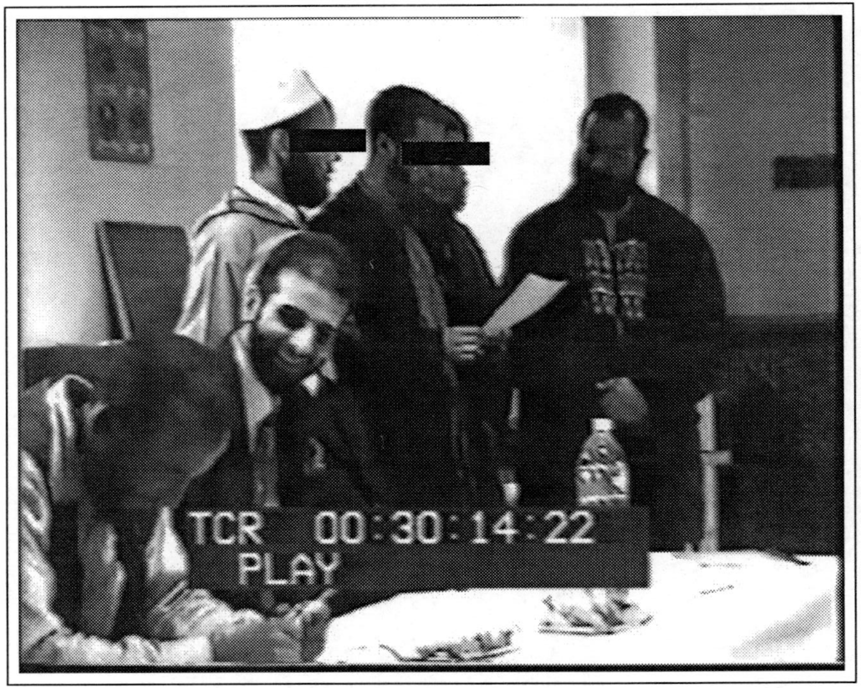

Figure 3. *The Quartet is Singing.*
Sitting: Ramzi Binalshibh and Said Bahaji. Standing to the right: Marwan al-Shehhi.

a Turkish imam from another Hamburg mosque delivers a short and quite unremarkable address in Arabic, expressing his best wishes to the couple. Later still, an Arabic wedding song is sung by a quartet. Afterwards a Moroccan imam gives a speech in Arabic on some aspects of marriage, and the procession of the guests congratulating the bridegroom and his father-in-law concludes the video.

2. *Jihadist Elements in the Wedding Ceremony*

These conventional elements are interspersed with scenes of a decidedly Jihadist character which, for the outside observer, are hardly compatible with the occasion of a wedding. Specifically, these scenes are:

1. a three-minute political speech by Ramzi Binalshibh, including a poem by the Syrian poet 'Umar Abū Rīsha (1910–90) which bears the title 'After the Catastrophe' (*Ba'd al-nakba*);
2. a battle-song, about five minutes long, encouraging the 'adherents of monotheism' to fight 'heresy';
3. a second political statement by Binalshibh, about one and a half minutes long, in which he mentions the glorious conquest of Constantinople in 1453 and says that colonialists and orientalists later succeeded in sowing the seeds of discord among the Muslims;
4. a song of five and a half minutes duration, praising military activity as the Muslim's real way of serving his God;
5. another song of four minutes length on the delights of dying as a martyr.

Of particular interest are the songs in scenes 4 and 5, as they represent a genre of religiously imbued music that apparently plays an enormous role in Jihadist circles. I leave aside the battle-song of scene 2, because its religious focus is not particularly evident. In fact, the two notions of *banū al-tawḥīd* 'adherents of monotheism' and *ilḥād* 'heresy' are the only religious terms in it, and they are comparatively vague.

3. *A Jihad Poem from the Eighth Century Set to Music*

A translation of the song is presented first, followed by an explanation. The wording of the song in scene 4 is as follows:

1. O 'Servant of the two Holy Places', if you saw us, you would know that you are only playing in your worship!
2. Others may tinge their cheeks with tears: our throats are tinged with our blood.

3. Others may exhaust their horses for idle purposes: our horses are worn out during the morning encounter with the enemy.
4. You smell of perfume, but our perfume is the dust stirred up by hooves, and the dust is the better perfume.
5. From the sayings of our Prophet, there has come down to us a reliable, truthful word which does not lie:
6. 'A man will never smell both the dust of God's cavalry and the smoke of a blazing fire [in hell]'.[252]
7. This is God's book, speaking among us, and it does not lie when saying 'the martyr is not dead'.[253]

The words of this song are a poem by 'Abdallāh Ibn Mubārak (d. AD 797) who was a transmitter of Prophetic tradition and is regarded as one of the founders of Sufism. He took part in several jihad campaigns and wrote a famous book on that topic, his *Kitāb al-Jihād.* The poem is addressed to another Sufi and expert on the Prophetic tradition named al-Fuḍayl Ibn 'Iyāḍ (d. AD 803) who was called 'Servant of the Two Holy Places'.[254] The text of the poem is related in the Koran commentary by Ibn Kathīr (d. AD 1373), where it is quoted to elucidate verse 200 of surah 3. It is composed in the classical *Kāmil* metre. During the wedding, one of the singers first reads out the words of the poem; afterwards, the quartet sings it with numerous repetitions. A much more professional version of the song can be found on the Internet.[255]

4. *A Modern Martyr Song*

The song in scene 5 reads as follows:

1. I wished life as a delight, as travel and struggle,
2. and I chose my path myself and moved forward fast on it,
3. and I became a fire and a light and… [?] and a perfume,
4. until I died as a martyr, welcoming the fate of death.
5. The light fills my eyes, and the paradise virgins sit in the grasp of my right hand,
6. and I sing like an angel amidst gardens and springs.
7. These gardens are my abode, and my wounds are its perfume;
8. enchantment, joy and wine: what a fine place of rest!
9. My fellows are the prophets and my brothers are the (other) martyrs,
10. and God bestows on us the shadows of a merciful love.
11. In God's gardens I live in a thousand and one worlds,
12. and anything I desire is brought to me swiftly.

13. Don't say about those who went away yesterday: We lost them!
14. If dwelling in the Garden of Eternity means being lost, then it is better that you should lose me.

The text is composed in the classical *Mujtathth* metre, but, as the rhyme shows, it is of modern origin. The song can be downloaded from the same website as the preceding one; the version to be found there is striking because of the singer's androgynous voice and the strange pronunciation of the Arabic letter *rā'*. At the wedding, it is sung by a trio.

5. *A Conservative Scholar's Approval of Singing* nashīd*s*

Songs like these two are called *nashīd* or *unshūda* in Arabic; the plural forms are *nashā'id*, *anshād* and *anāshīd*. If the form *nashīd* or *anāshīd* is typed into a search engine (in Arabic characters, of course), the result is a huge number of hits yielding either song lyrics, or, more often, audio files. Not all *nashīd*s display such a Jihadist character as the two examples sung at Bahaji's wedding. A *nashīd* may have a non-political and non-religious character; the semantic core of the term is just 'song, hymn'. But in a narrower sense, *nashīd* is a political or religious (or religio-political) song.[256] The volume of examples of this special type that is accessible on the Web is so large that it could be subject of more than one doctoral dissertation.

Although Islamic civilization developed a rich heritage of music, orthodox circles always had strong objections to various modes of musical activity. The best-known and most extreme example is the Taliban regime's complete ban on music in Afghanistan. Therefore, it is not surprising that the conformity of the *nashīd*s (or *unshūda*s) with 'true Islam' has been discussed. For example, on the previously mentioned website, Islaam.net, the ruling of the Salafī scholar Nāṣir al-Dīn al-Albānī[257] is quoted, obviously to ease concerns about the 'Islamic admissibility' of these songs. It reads:

> If these nashîds have 'Islamic' meanings whilst not having in them any musical instruments such as duffs, other drums, or the like, then there is no problem in this. However, it is necessary to explain an important prerequisite for their permissibility, and that is that they should be free of anything contradicting the shari'ah such as excessiveness and the like. Then another condition is that it should not become a habit because that diverts listeners [of the nashîds] from the recitation of the Qur'ân, which is encouraged in the Prophetic, purified, sunnah. Likewise, it diverts them from seeking beneficial knowledge and calling to Allâh subhanahu. As for the use of duffs in nashids, then this is permissible for women when amongst themselves, and not for men, and on 'îd and on weddings only.

Indeed, both songs in their more professional versions on the Web as well as in their renditions at the wedding are purely vocal music.

6. *Insider Assessments of the History and Function of* nashīds

On 27 September 2003, the Arabic newspaper *Asharq Al-Awsat*[258] published an article by Muḥammad al-Shāfiʿī entitled 'Dispute among fundamentalists on the use of files on "The Black-eyed Virgins" for the mobilization of the fighters of al-Qaeda'.[259] Here is a translation of the most important paragraphs of this well-informed article:

> A dispute has arisen among fundamentalists (*uṣūliyyūn*) about the recent release of data bearing the name 'The Black-eyed Virgins' (*al-ḥūr al-ʿīn*). This is the designation of three audio files by a number of scholars belonging to fundamentalist organizations in the Gulf region. Their aim is to promote mobilization of fighters for al-Qaeda. The 'Jihad Club' (*al-Muntadā al-jihādī*) posted these files on the site *Balsam al-Īmān* ('The Balm of Faith') the day before yesterday.[260] Other websites close to al-Qaeda disseminated the files, which exhort Muslims to renounce the world and direct their hopes to the beauty of the paradise virgins… The propagandists concentrate their efforts on depicting these virgins and the delight awaiting the martyrs.
>
> The three files were produced by someone who calls himself 'The Eastern Scholar' (*al-ṭālib al-sharqī*), which is the alias of a fundamentalist leader close to al-Qaeda. He is the very person who formerly produced files bearing the name 'Jihad is your duty' (*ʿalaykum bi-l-jihād*).
>
> The Libyan Islamist (*islāmī*) Nuʿmān Ibn ʿUthmān told Asharq Alawsat in a phone conversation that fundamentalists have collected such files since the days of Afghanistan. The expert on fundamentalist movements added that in about 90 per cent of the cases the incentive for the Mujahid to sacrifice his life is the expected reward in the Hereafter, especially the joy found with the paradise virgins…
>
> ʿUmar al-Bakrī, leader of the movement *al-Muhājirūn*, the largest fundamentalist organization in Britain, told Asharq Alawsat that the Islamists have been repeating their *nashīd*s for 25 years and dream day and night (of paradise), saying 'The light fills my eyes, and the paradise virgins sit in the grasp of my right hand, and I am like an angel singing amidst gardens and springs'.[261] The Syrian fundamentalist explained that 'the audio files come under the heading of inciting interest in jihad, of instigating and impelling to it'. He added that those who belong to Jihadist circles know the descriptions of the paradise virgins by heart, as they are based on Koranic passages and Prophetic tradition. He said that the mujahedin in Iraq, Afghanistan and Chechnya long primarily for paradise with its virgins, its rivers, milk and honey…[262]

> [Dr Hānī al-Sibā'ī, an Islamist who hails from Egypt and directs the al-Maqrīzī Institute in London] said that there is one famous paradise virgin called al-'Aynā', for whom all fighters of al-Qaeda long and whom they desire for themselves. If she unveiled her face, the light of it would extinguish the sun...[263]

7. *Conclusions*

The wedding ceremony was an event that brought together some important members of the Hamburg group and a wider public. Many guests are sure to have had their reservations about its radical Jihadist ring. But although the missionary character of the event is obvious, we may assume that the ritual of singing was an important element for bringing about coherence within the Hamburg group itself. Songs about jihad, martyrdom and houris were composed, sung and recorded from the early days of the war against the Soviets in Afghanistan. In former days, these songs were distributed in cassette form; nowadays, the Web facilitates the spread of this means of propaganda and recruitment to an extent that was inconceivable as recently as the early 1990s. The high technical standard of these files and their undeniable aesthetic value will only add to their suggestive effect. And the paradise virgins are as present in this sort of poetry set to music as they are in the *Spiritual Manual*.

8. *Arabic Text of the Songs*

The song in scene 4:

1.	*yā 'ābida l-ḥaramayni law abṣartanā*	*la-'alimta annaka bi-l-'ibādati tal'abū*
2.	*man kāna yakhḍibu khaddahū bi-dumū'ihī*	*fa-nuḥūrunā bi-dimā'inā tatakhaḍḍabū*
3.	*aw kāna yut'ibu khaylahū fī bāṭilin*	*fa-khuyūlunā yawma l-ṣabīḥati tat'abū*
4.	*rīḥu l-'abīri lakum wa-naḥnu 'abīrunā*	*wahaju l-sanābiki wa-l-ghubāru l-aṭyabū*
5.	*wa-la-qad atānā min maqāli nabiyyinā*	*qawlun ṣaḥīḥun ṣādiqun lā yakdhibū*
6.	*lā yastawī wa-ghubāru khayli llāhi fī*	*anfi mri'in wa-dukhānu nārin tulhabū*
7.	*hādhā kitābu llāhi yanṭiqu baynanā*	*laysa l-shahīdu bi-mayyitin lā yakdhibū*

The order in which the lines are sung is: 1, 2, 1, 2, 3, 3, 4, 1, 2, 5, 5, 6, 1, 2, 7, 7, 7, 1, 2.

The song in scene 5:

1.	*shi'tu l-ḥayāta matā'an*	*wa-riḥlatan wa-ṣirā'an*
2.	*wa-khtartu darbī bi-nafsī*	*wa-sirtu fīhi sirā'an*
3.	*wa-ṣirtu nāran wa-nūran*	*wa-ghinwatan wa-'abīran*
4.	*ḥattā qaḍaytu shahīdan*	*muraḥḥiban bi-l-manūni*
5.	*al-nūru mil'u 'uyūnī*	*wa-l-ḥūru milku yamīnī*
6.	*wa-ka-l-malāki ughannī*	*fī jannatin wa-'uyūnin*
7.	*hādhī l-jinānu marāḥī*	*wa-'iṭruhā min jirāḥī*
8.	*siḥrun wa-rawḥun wa-rāḥun*	*yā qalbu ayyu rawāḥin*
9.	*jullāsiya l-anbiyā'u*	*wa-ikhwatī l-shuhadā'u*
10.	*wa-llāhu yulqī 'alaynā*	*ẓilāla ḥubbin ḥanūnin*
11.	*fī jannati llāhi aḥyā*	*fī alfi dunyā wa-dunyā*
12.	*wa-mā tamannaytu shay'an*	*illā atānī sarī'an*
13	*fa-lā taqūlū khasirnā*	*man ghāba bi-l-amsi 'annā*
14.	*in kāna fī l-khuldi khusrun*	*fa-l-khayru an takhsarūnī*

The first word of line 8, *siḥrun*, is taken from the text and audio versions available on the Internet; on the video, some other word is sung which I could not identify. *sarī'an* in line 12 is taken from the text version on the Internet; on the video as well as in the audio version from the Web, *sarī'an* is definitively not sung. The order in which the lines are sung is: 1, 1, 2, 2, 3, 3, 4, 4, 5, 5, 6, 6 (second half), 7, 7, 8, 8, 9, 9, 10, 10, 5, 5, 6, 6 (second half), 11, 11, 12, 12, 13, 13, 14, 14 (second half), 14 (second half).

9

THE ARABIC TEXT OF THE *SPIRITUAL MANUAL*

Tilman Seidensticker, Albrecht Fuess and Moez Khalfaoui

The following edition is based on two sources:

1. the scanned versions to be found on the web: Bearing the mark 'FBI Laboratory 010918019 K 655', these documents seem to have been scanned from the original handwritten version which was on two sheets of paper fastened by a staple in the upper right corner of the odd pages;
2. a photocopy of a different version which formed part of the evidence used in the trial against Mounir Motassadeq at the *Hanseatisches Oberlandesgericht* in Hamburg, Germany. This document bears the mark 'FBI Laboratory K70 010917003 HC' and must be a photocopy of the original text on four pages.

In our edition, we have retained the orthography of the original text as far as possible, even with respect to the writing or omitting of *hamza* and the dotting of final *yā'*.[264] Only in the case of undotted *tā' marbūṭa* have we supplied the two dots. All our additions appear in square brackets, the only exception being in item 12 of page 1 where the scribe used square brackets himself. These brackets have been marked in bold font. When the orthography or syntax of the text differs from Modern Standard Arabic, we have normally inserted an exclamation mark in square brackets.

The subdivision of the text into paragraphs exactly follows the original. To make the translation easier to read, we provide a new subdivision into numbered paragraphs for pages 2 to 4. This division is indicated in the Arabic text by small Arabic numerals in square brackets, e.g. [1]. 'Genuine' Arabic numerals in square brackets, separated by a comma, indicate quotations from the Koran. [٤٦،٨], for example, means that the preceding quotation is from surah 8 verse 46 in the Cairo standard edition of 1924.

Page 1:

الليلة الأخيرة :

١ – التبايع على الموت وتجديد النية

حلق الشعر الزائد من الجسم والتطييب

الاغتسال

٢ – معرفة الخطة جيداً من كل النواحي وتوقع ردة الفعل أو المقاومة من العدو

٣ – قراءة سورة التوبة والانفال وتدبر معانيه [!] وما أعده الله للمؤمنين من النعيم المقيم للشهداء

٤ – تذكير النفس بالسمع والطاعة تلك الليلة فانك ستتعرض لمواقف حاسمة لا بد فيها من السمع والطاعة (١٠٠ ٪) فروض نفسك وفهمها وأقنعها وحرّضها على ذلك قال تعالى (وأطيعوا الله ورسوله ولا تنازعوا فتفشلوا وتذهب ريحكم واصبروا إن الله مع الصابرين [٨،٤٦]

٥ – قيام الليل والإلحاح فى الدعاء بالنصر والتمكين والفتح المبين وتيسير الأمور والستر علينا

٦ – كثرة الذكر واعلموا أن خير الذكر قراءة القرآن الكريم وذلك بإجماع أهل العلم فيما أعلم و يكفى لنا انه كلام فاطر السموات والأرض الذى أنت مقبل عليه

٧ – صف قلبك ونقه من الشوائب وانسى [!] وتناسى [!] شيء [!] اسمه دنيا فقد مضى زمن اللعب وجاء الموعد الحق وكم ضيعنا من أعمارنا من أوقات أفلا نستغل تلك الساعات لتقديم القربات والطاعات

٨ – ليكن صدرك منشرحاً فإنه ما بينك وبين زواجك إلا لحظات يسيرة بها تبدأ الحياة السعيدة الرضية والنعيم الخالد مع النبيين والصديقين والشهداء والصالحين وحسن أولئك رفيقاً [٦٩،٤] نسأل الله من فضله وكن متفائلاً فإنه عليه الصلاة والسلام (كان يحب الفأل فى أمره كله)

٩ – ثم اجعل نصب عينيك أنك اذا وقعت فى ابتلاء كيف تتصرف وكيف تثبت وتسترجع وتعلم أن ما أصابك لم يكن ليخطئك وما أخطئك [!] لم يكن ليصيبك وأن هذا الابتلاء من الله جل وعلا ليرفع درجتك ويكفر عن ذنوبك ثم اعلم أنه لحظات ثم ينجلي بإذن الله فيا هنيئًا لمن فاز بالأجر العظيم من الله قال تعالى (أم حسبتم أن تدخلو [!] الجنة ولما يعلم الله الذين جاهدوا منكم ويعلم الصابرين) [١٤٢،٣]

١٠ – ثم تذكروا قول الله تعالى (ولقد كنتم تمنون الموت من قبل أن تلقوه فقد رأيتموه وأنتم تنظرون ... الاية) [١٤٣،٣] وبعد ذلك تذكروا (كم من فئة قليلة غلبت فئة كثيرة بإذن الله ... الاية) [٢٤٩،٢] وقوله تعالى (إن ينصركم الله فلا غالب لكم وإن يخذلكم فمن ذا الذي ينصركم من بعده وعلى الله فليتوكل المؤمنون) [١٦٠،٣]

١١ – ذكر نفسك بالأدعية وإخوانك وتدبر ما معانيها (أذكار الصباح والمساء – اذكار البلدة واذكار المكان وأذكار لقاء العدو الخ)

١٢ – النفث [على النفس – والشنطة – والملابس – والسكين – أدواتك – بطاقتك – (تذ) – جوازك – أوراقك كلها]

١٣ – تفقد سلاحك قبل الرحيل وقبل قبل الرحيل و (ليحد أحدكم شفرته وليرح ذبيحته)
١٤ – شد عليك ملابسك جيدًا وهذا هو نهج السلف الصالح رضوان الله عليهم وكانو [!] يشدون ملابسهم عليهم قبل المعركة ثم وشد حذائك [!] جيدًا ولبس [!] شرابًا يكون تمسك في الحذاء ولا تخرج منه وهذه كلها أسباب مأمورون [!] بالأخذ بها وحسبنا الله ونعم الوكيل [١٧٣،٣]
١٥ – صل الصبح فى جماعة وتدبر أجرها وائت بالاذكار بعدها ولا تخرج من شقتك إلا متوضئا فإن الملائكة تستغفر لك ما دمت متوضئا وتدعوا [!] لك واقرء [!] قول الله تعالى (أفحسبتم أنما خلقناكم عبثا ... الاية) (سورة المؤمنون) [١١٥،٢٣]

On top of page 1, probably belonging to § 3:

قال أحد الصحابة أمرنا رسول الله بقراءتها قبل الغزوة فقرأناها فغنمنا وسلمنا

Under page 1, probably belonging to the text immediately preceding:

[...] الحديث المذكور ذكره النووى فى كتابه المختار من الاذكار الملاحظة [... ...]

Page 2:

بعد ذلك المرحلة الثانية

[1] اذا تقلك التكسي إلى (م) فاذكر الله في [؟] السيارة ذكر [!] كثيراً (ذكر الركوب – ذكر البلدة – ذكر المكان الاذكار الأخرى)

[2] اذا وصلت ورأيت (م) ونزلت من التاكسي فقل دعاء المكان وكل مكان تذهب قل فيه دعاء المكان وابتسم واطمئن فإن الله مع المؤمنين والملائكة تحرسك وأنت لا تشعر

[3] ثم قل دعاء (الله أعز من خلقه جميعاً [...]) وقل (اللهم أكفناهم بما شئت) وقل (اللهم إنا ندرأ بك فى نحورهم ونعوذ بك من شرورهم وقل (اللهم اجعل لنا من بين أيديهم سدا ومن خلفهم سدا وأغشهم فهم لا يبصرون [cf. ٣٦،٩] وقل (حسبنا الله ونعم الوكيل) [٣،١٧٣] [4] مستحضراً قوله تعالى(الذين قال لهم الناس إن الناس قد جمعوا لكم فاخشوهم فزادهم إيماناً وقالو [!] حسبنا الله ونعم الوكيل) [٣،١٧٣]

[5] فإنك بعدما تقوله سوف تجد أمور [!] تتدبر [... ... ...] لأن الله قد وعد عباده الذين يقولون هذا الدعاء بما يلى:

١ – الانقلاب بنعمة الله وفضله

٢ – لم يمسهم سوء

٣ – اتباع رضوان الله

[6] قال تعالى (فانقلبوا بنعمة من الله وفضل لم يمسسهم سوء واتبعوا رضوان الله والله ذو فضل عظيم) [٣،١٧٤] فإن أجهزتهم وأبوابهم وتكنلوجيتهم كلها لا تنفع ولا تضر إلا بإذن الله

[7] ولا يخاف منها المؤمنون وانما يخاف منها أولياء الشيطان الذين هم فى الأصل يخافون الشيطان وأصبحو [!] من أولياءه والعياذ بالله فإن الخوف عبادة عظيم [!] لا تصرف إلا لله سبحانه وتعالى وهو أحق بها [8] قال تعالى معقباً على تلك الايات (إنما ذلكم الشيطان يخوف أولياءه) [٣،١٧٥] المعجبين بحضارة الغرب الذين شربوا حبهم وتقديسهم [؟] مع الماء البارد وخافوا من معداتهم الضعيفة الواهية (فلا تخافوهم وخافون إن كنتم مؤمنين) [٣،١٧٥] فإن الخوف عبادة عظيم [!] أولياء الله والمؤمنون لا يصرفونها إلا لله الواحد الأحد الذي بيده كل شيء وموقنين [؟] أشد اليقين أن الله سيبطل كيد الكافرين فقد قال تعالى (ذلكم وأن الله موهن كيد الكافرين) [٨،١٨] [9] ثم عليكم بذكر [...] من أعظم الذكر وخاصة يجب ألا يلاحظ عليك أنك تذكر قول (لا إله إلا الله) فإنك لو قلتها ألف مرة ما استطاع أحد أن يميز هل أنت ساكت أم تذكر الله [10] ومن عظمها قوله عليه الصلاة والسلام (من قال لا إله إلا الله مومن بها قلبه دخل الجنة) أو كما قال قال عليه الصلاة والسلام فى معناه (لو وضعت السموات السبع والارضين السبع فى كفة ولا إله إلا الله فى كفة لرجحت بهن لا إله إلا الله) [11] وتستطيع أن تبتسم وأنت تقولها وهذا من عظم هذه الكلمة والمتأمل فيها يجد حروفها غير منقوطة وهذا من كمال عظمتها حيث إن [!] الكلمات أو الحروف المنقوطة

أقل من غيرها [12] ويكفي أنها كلمة التوحيد الذي أنت أتيت لرفعها والقتال تحت رايتها كما فعل الرسول صلى الله عليه وسلم وصحابته ومن تبعهم بإحسان الى يوم الدين

Page 3:

[13] وأيضاً لا تظهر عليك مظاهر الارتباك وشد الاعصاب وكن فرحاً سعيداً منشرح الصدر مطمئن [!] لانك تقوم بعمل يحبه الله ويرضاه ومن ثم سوف يكون يوم بإذن الله تقضيه مع الحور العين فى الجنة

[14] تبسم بوجه الردى يا فتى فإنك ماضٍ لجنات خلد

[15] أي مكان تذهب إليه أو أي فعل تقوم عليكً بالذكر والدعاء والله مع عباده المؤمنين بالحفظ والتيسير والتوفيق والتمكين والنصر وكل شيء

المرحلة الثالثة:

[1] عندما تركب (ط) أول ما تضع رجلك وقبل ما تدخلها تأتي بالدعاء والأدعية واستحضر أنها غزوة في سبيل [!] أو كما قال عليه الصلاة والسلام (لغدوة أو روحة فى سبيل الله خير من الدنيا وما فيها) أو كما قال عليه الصلاة والسلام [2] وعندما تضع رجلك في (ط) وتجلس على كرسيك فقل الاذكار وأئت [!] بالادعية المعروفة التى ذكرناها سابقاً ثم كن منشغلاً بذكر الله والاكثار منه [3] قال تعالى (يا أيها الذين آمنوا إذا لقيتم فئة فاثبتوا واذكروا الله كثيراً لعلكم تفلحون) [٨،٤٥] [4] ثم اذا

تحركت (ط) حركة البسيط [!] واصبحت تتوجه إلى (ق) فقل دعاء السفر فإنك مسافر إلى الله تعالى (وانعم بهذا السفر)

[5] ثم ستجدها تقف ثم تنطلق وهذه هي ساعة إلتقاء الصفان [!] فادعوا الله تعالى كما ذكر تعالى في كتابه (اللهم [! ربنا Qur'ān:] أفرغ علينا صبرا وثبت أقدامنا وانصرنا على القوم الكافرين) [٢٥٠،٢] وقوله تعالى (وما كان قولهم إلا أن قالوا ربنا اغفر لنا ذنوبنا واسرافنا في أمرنا وثبت أقدامنا وانصرنا على القوم الكافرين) [١٤٧،٣] [6] وقول نبيه عليه الصلاة والسلام (اللهم منزل الكتاب مجري السحاب هازم الاحزاب اهزمهم وانصرنا عليهم اللهم اهزمهم وزلزلهم) [7] ادعوا [!] لنفسك ولإخوانك كلهم بالفتح والنصر واصابة الهدف ولا تخاف[!] واطلب من الله أن يرزقك الشهادة مقبلاً غير مدبر صابراً محتسبا

[8] ثم ليستعد كل واحد منكم للقيام بدوره على الوجه الذي يرضى الله عنه وليشد على أسنانه كما كان يفعل السلف رحمهم الله قبل الاشتباك في المعركة

[9] وعند الالتحام فضرب [!] ضرب الابطال الذين لا يريدون الرجوع إلى الدنيا وكبر فإن التكبير يدخل الرعب فى قلوب الكافرين فقال تعالى (فاضربوا فوق الاعناق واضربوا منهم كل بنان) [١٢،٨] [10] واعلموا أن الجنان قد تزينت لكم بأجلى حللها والحور تناديكم أن أقبل يا ولي الله وهي قد لبست أحسن حللها

[11] واذا من الله على أحدكم بالذبح فلينوها عن أبيه وأمه فإن لهما حقاً عليك ولا تختلفوا واسمعوا وأطيعوا واذا ذبحتم فاسلبوا من تقتلوه لان ذلك سنة من سنن المصطفى صلى الله عليه وسلم ولكن

بشرط ألا ينشغل بالسلب ويترك ما هو أعظم من الانتباه للعدو وخيانته أو هجومه فإن ذلك ضرره أعظم [12] فإن كان كذلك

Page 4:

فتقديم مصلحة العمل والجماعة مقدم على فعل هذه السنة لان العمل فرض عليه وهذا سنة والواجب مقدم على السنة [13] ولا تنتقم لنفسك ولكن اجعل ضربك وكل شيء لله تعالى فهذا على بن أبي طالب رضى الله عنه تعارك هو احد الكفار فقام الكافر (فبصق) على عليّ رضى الله عنه فأوقف سيفه ولم يضربه ثم ضربه [14] فلما انتهت المعركة سئله [!] الصحابة عن فعله هذا ولماذا لم يضرب هذا الكافر وتركه ثم ضربه فقال على رضى الله عنه (لما بصق علي خشيت أن أضربه إنتقاماً لنفسي فرجعت سيفى) او كما قال [15] ثم لما استحضر النية قام فضربه فقضى عليه وهذا كله يعنى في مدة يسيرة يوطن الانسان نفسه من قبل أن يكون عمله لله كله

[16] ثم طبقوا سنة الأسر وأسروا منهم واقتلوهم كما قال تعالى (ما كان لنبيّ أن يكون له أسرى حتى يثخن في الأرض تريدون عرض الدنيا والله يريد الآخرة والله عزيز حكيم) [٦٧،٨]

[17] اذا تم كل شيء على ما يرام فكل واحد منكم يضرب على كتف أخيه من الشقة وفى (م) وفى (ط) وفي (ك) يذكره أن هذا العمل لله جل وعلا ولا يربك اخوانه أو يشوش عليهم بل يبشرهم ويطمئنهم ويذكرهم ويشجعهم [18] وما أجمل لو قرا

الانسان أيات [!] من القرآن مثل قوله تعالى (فليقاتل في سبيل الله الذين يشرون الحياة الدنيا بالآخرة ... الاية) [٤،٧٤]
وقوله تعالى (ولا تحسبن الذين قتلوا فى سبيل الله امواتا ... الاية) [٣،١٦٩]
وغيرها [19] أو ينشد لهم كما كان السلف يرتجزون وسط المعارك ليطمئن اخوانه ويدخل على قلوبهم السكينة والفرح
[20] ولا تنسو [!] الأخذ من الغنيمة ولو فنجان أو كاسة من الماء تسقي نفسك و إخوانك إن تيسر [21] ثم اذا اقترب الوعد الحق وجاءت ساعة الصفر
فشق بدلتك وافتح صدرك مرحبا بالموت فى سبيل الله [22] وكن دائماً ذاكراً و إما أن تختتم بالصلاة أن تيسر تشرع فيها قبل الهدف بثواني [!] أو يكون آخر كلامك لا إله إلا الله محمد رسول الله

[23] وبعدها إنشاء الله اللقاء فى الفردوس الأعلى برحمة الله

Following immediately, but marked with an asterisk and obviously without relation to the preceding text:

اذا رأيت جموع الكفر فتذكر الأحزاب الذين كان عددهم ما يقارب ١٠٠٠٠ آلاف مقاتل وكيف نصر الله عباده المؤمنين
قال تعالى (ولما رأى المؤمنون الاحزاب قالوا هذا ما وعدنا الله ورسوله وصدق الله ورسوله وما زادهم الا ايمانا وتسليما) الاية [٣٣،٢٢]

وصلى الله على نبينا محمد

Endnotes

1. See online: http://www.fbi.gov/pressrel/pressrel01/letter.html (accessed 22 August 2006).

2. *The 9/11 Commission Report: Final Report of the National Commission on Terrorist Attacks upon the United States* (New York: W. W. Norton, 2004), p. 1; cf. n. 21.

3. English translation by Terry McDermott, *Perfect Soldiers: The Hijackers; Who they were, Why they did it* (New York: HarperCollins, 2005), pp. 245-47.

4. See online: http://www.observer.co.uk/international/story/0,6903,560773,00.html (accessed 22 August 2006). The document was translated by Imad Musa, a translator of the Capital Communications Group, a Washington-based international consulting firm.

5. Hassan Mneimneh, 'Appendix', in Robert B. Silvers and Barbara Epstein (eds.), *Striking Terror: America's New War* (New York: New York Review of Books, 2002), pp. 319-27.

6. David Cook, *Understanding Jihad* (Berkeley: University of California Press, 2005), pp. 195-202, with notes pp. 233-35.

7. 'Translated Text: Hijackers' How-To', *CBS News* (1 October 2001), online: http://www.cbsnews.com/stories/2001/10/01/archive/main313163.shtml (accessed 22 August 2006).

8. Yosri Fouda and Nick Fielding, *Masterminds of Terror: The Truth behind the most Devastating Terrorist Attack the World has ever Seen* (Edinburgh: Mainstream, 2003), p. 115. Cf. also p. 141.

9. 1/6, emphasis HGK.

10. *The 9/11 Commission Report*, pp. 232-33 with notes (abbreviated by HGK).

11. Robert Fisk: 'What Muslim would Write: 'The time of fun and waste is gone'?', *The Independent* (29 September 2001). As additional evidence he cites the expressions '100 per cent' and 'optimistic', as being too modern for Arabic theological language. Fisk drew a cautious conclusion about possible Christian translators: 'The translation, as it stands, suggests an almost Christian view of what the hijackers might have felt'.

12. Michael Barkun, *A Culture of Conspiracy: Apocalyptic Visions in Contemporary America* (Berkeley: University of California Press, 2003), Chapter 10 ('September 11: The Aftermath'); other conspiracy narratives are reported by Malise Ruthven, *A Fury for God: The Islamist Attack on America* (London: Granada, 2002), pp. 294-98.

13. John L. Esposito, *Unholy War: Terror in the Name of Islam* (Oxford: Oxford University Press, 2002), p. 74; the Anti-Defamation League refuted the rumours (see 'Unravelling Anti-Semitic 9/11 Conspiracy Theories', online: http://www.adl.org/anti_semitism/9-11conspiracytheories.pdf [accessed 22 August 2006]).

14. 'Unravelling Anti-Semitic 9/11 Conspiracy Theories', p. 20.

15. Some of the more private documents are collected by Barry Rubin and Judith Colp Rubin (eds.), *Anti-American Terrorism and the Middle East: A Documentary*

Reader (Oxford: Oxford University Press, 2002), pp. 243-67; in public Usama bin Ladin claimed full responsibility in a video address to the American nation on the eve of the 2004 presidential elections; see Bruce Lawrence (ed.), *Messages to the World: The Statements of Osama bin Laden* (trans. James Howarth; London/New York: Verso 2005), pp. xiv-xv and pp. 237-44 (Statement 23).

16. Rubin and Rubin (eds.), *Anti-American Terrorism and the Middle East*, p. 276.

17. Cook, *Understanding Jihad*, pp. 175-81.

18. An exception is the volume by Michael Czogalla (ed.), *The Political and Spiritual Motivations of the 9/11 Attackers* (Washington: Friedrich-Ebert-Stiftung, 2005).

19. See n. 2, above.

20. *The 9/11 Commission Report*, p. 253.

21. 'Outline of the 9/11 Plot', Staff Statement No. 16, p. 11; published online: http://www.9-11commission.gov/staff_statements/staff_statement_16.pdf (accessed 22 August 2006).

22. *The 9/11 Commission Report*, p. xvi.

23. A footnote explains: 'For purposes of this definition, the term "noncombatant" is interpreted to include, in addition to civilians, military personnel who at the time of the incident are unarmed or not on duty... We also consider as acts of terrorism attacks on military installations or on armed military'.

24. Robert Kennedy, 'Is One Person's Terrorist Another's Freedom Fighter? Western and Islamic Approaches to 'Just War' Compared', *Terrorism and Political Violence* 11 (1999), pp. 1-21.

25. Tomis Kapitan, 'The Terrorism of "Terrorism"', in James Sterba (ed.), *Terrorism and International Justice* (New York/Oxford: Oxford University Press, 2003), pp. 47-66.

26. Mark Danner, *Torture and Truth: America, Abu Ghraib, and the War on Terror* (New York: New York Review of Books, 2004), pp. 105-106.

27. Hassan Mneimneh and Kanan Makiya, 'Manual for a "Raid"', *New York Review of Books* (17 January 2002; online: http://www.nybooks.com/articles/15106 [accessed 22 August 2006]). Repr. in Silvers and Epstein (eds.): *Striking Terror*, pp. 301-18.

28. See online: http://marty-center.uchicago.edu/webforum/122002/index.shtml (accessed 22 August 2006).

29. Yvonne Y. Haddad, 'Sayyid Qutb: Ideologue of Islamic Revival', in John L. Esposito (ed.), *Voices of Resurgent Islam* (New York/Oxford: Oxford University Press, 1983), pp. 67-98; Emmanuel Sivan, *Radical Islam: Medieval Theology and Modern Politics* (New Haven: Yale University Press, 2nd edn, 1990), pp. 21-28.

30. Hans G. Kippenberg and Tilman Seidensticker (eds.), *Terror im Dienste Gottes: Die 'Geistliche Anleitung' der Attentäter des 11. September 2001* (Frankfurt: Campus, 2004).

31. The translation is based on the German translation by Albrecht Fuess, Moez Khalfaoui, and Tilman Seidensticker, in Kippenberg and Seidensticker (eds.), *Terror im Dienste Gottes*, pp. 17-27. The English translation was carried out by Tilman Seidensticker and Hans G. Kippenberg and refers to the amended Arabic text published in this volume. Some footnotes were added by Tilman Seidensticker. The

translations of Koranic citations are taken from the translation by Arthur J. Arberry (*The Koran Interpreted: A Translation* [New York: Simon & Schuster, 1996]; originally published in two volumes [London: Allen & Unwin; New York: Macmillan, 1955]). The divergent numbers of the verses are adapted to the numbering of the Cairo standard edition of 1924.

32. *niyya* ('intention') is a technical term in Islamic law. Formulating the intention to perform an act which is prescribed by Islamic law is a prerequisite for the validity of this act.

33. The last sentence is written at the top of the first page and probably is an addition to the command to recite surahs 9 and 8. According to another addition at the bottom of the page, the quoted saying of the Prophet is taken from the book *al-Mukhtār min al-adhkār* ('Selected prayers') by al-Nawawī (d. AD 1277).

34. We translate the Arabic noun *nafs* in *fa-rawwiḍ nafsaka wa-fahhimhā*...as a reflexive pronoun. It could also be understood as 'soul' in the Ṣūfic tradition, so that the sentence would mean: 'Pull your soul together, make it understand, convince it and incite it to this action'.

35. 'Prayer' here refers to the Arabic noun *du'ā'* (plural *ad'iya*). In other places (but not always), we translate the word *dhikr* (plural *adhkār*) as 'prayer' as well. On the semantic differences between the two words, cf. Tilman Seidensticker's first contribution to this volume, pp. 19-27 (21).

36. *ijmā'* ('consensus [of the scholars]') is another technical term of Islamic law; it can be binding in cases where there is no ruling in the Koran or in Prophetic tradition.

37. This quotation is to be found in the canonical collections of Prophetic tradition, but with a different wording, which, moreover, shows that the prophet Muḥammad used the word *fa'l* in the sense of 'good omen'.

38. Prophetic tradition, cf. Arent Jan Wensinck *et al.*, *Concordance et indices de la tradition musulmane* (7 vols.; Leiden: Brill, 1936–69), II, p. 41b.

39. The word *nafth* 'spitting' alludes to a sort of magic (*ruqya*) that is said to have been practised even by the prophet Muḥammad. The first or the two last surahs of the Koran are recited, and afterwards the reciter spits into his palm and touches the person (or thing) to be cured or protected. On this practice in Prophetic tradition, see Wensinck *et al.*, *Concordance*, VI, pp. 497-98.

40. In the Arabic text, only the letters *tdh* are written, which are probably an abbreviation of *tadhkira* ('ticket').

41. The quotation is a Prophetic tradition on slaughtering; cf. Wensinck, *Concordance*, I, p. 430b.

42. In the Arabic text, only the letter *m* is written, which is presumably an abbreviation of the Arabic word *maṭār* ('airport').

43. The 'gates' might allude to the metal detectors in airports.

44. These words are the first part of the Islamic creed and mean 'there is no god but God'.

45. Prophetic tradition; cf. Muslim's *Ṣaḥīḥ*, Chapter *ṣalāt*, no. 12.

46. Prophetic tradition; cf. Wensinck *et al.*, *Concordance*, VI, p. 30b.

47. In the Arabic script, dots above or under letters serve to distinguish individual letters from each other. The first part of the Islamic creed is written only with letters that are not dotted.

48. Literally 'fewer', which is not true, nor does it seem to make any sense.

49. In the Arabic text, just the letter *ṭ* is written, which must be an abbreviation of *ṭā'ira* ('airplane').

50. Prophetic tradition; cf. Wensinck *et al.*, *Concordance*, IV, p. 465b.

51. In the Arabic text, only the letter *q* is written. It is uncertain which word is abbreviated in this way, but the sense is quite clear.

52. These 'factions' refer to the confederacy of the Muslims' enemies in the War of the Trench; see n. 56, below.

53. Prayer of the prophet Muḥammad; cf. Wensinck *et al.*, *Concordance*, I, p. 341b.

54. *sunna* ('custom') and *wājib* ('obligation') are technical terms of Islamic law.

55. 'Alī Ibn Abī Ṭālib was a cousin and son-in-law of the prophet Muḥammad and became fourth caliph from AD 656 to 661.

56. This episode is said to have happened during the so-called War of the Trench in AD 627 when the Muslims in Medina were attacked by an enormous force of the Meccans and their allies. Cf. 'Speech 53 of Imam Khomeini', online: www.irib.ir/worldservice/imam/speech/53.htm, or 'Jihad (Struggle)', online: www.islamic-city.com/islam/jihad.htm (accessed 22 August 2006). The Sunni historians report the killing of the Meccan 'Amr Ibn 'Abd Wudd by 'Alī but do not mention the incident of the spitting.

57. In the text, just the letter *k* is written, which might be an abbreviation of *kābīna* ('cockpit').

58. The ancient Arabic *rajaz* metre was used for extemporized battle poems. In his collection of prayers, al-Nawawī (cf. n. 33, above) included a 'Book on jihad prayers' (*Kitāb adhkār al-jihād*) within which there is a chapter 'Reciting *rajaz* poems during fighting is recommendable' (*Bāb istiḥbāb al-rajaz ḥāl al-mubāraza*). See Muḥyī al-Dīn Yaḥyā Ibn Sharaf al-Nawawī al-Dimashqī, *al-Adhkār al-nawawiyya* (no place, Edisoft, 2005), pp. 149-50.

59. This last paragraph seems to be an addition to some earlier part of the text. It refers to the War of the Trench, on which cf. n. 56.

60. Sentences in which such instructions are explained or substantiated by references to Islamic tradition and history are included in this figure.

61. For these prayers, cf. the second part of this contribution (pp. 22-23).

62. Cf. Seidensticker's third contribution to this volume (pp. 71-78).

63. Juan Cole, 'Al-Qaeda's Doomsday Document and Psychological Manipulation', online: http://www.juancole.com/essays/qaeda.htm (accessed 22 August 2006).

64. Hassan al-Bannâ, *Al Ma'thûrât. Invocations quotidiennes selon le Coran et la Sunna. Français–Arabe avec translittération phonétique. Préface de Tariq Ramadan* (Lyon: Tawhid, 2004).

65. The card is made of stiff, water-resistant cardboard and, if folded once, is no larger than an identity card or a driver's licence.

66. Fouda and Fielding, *Masterminds of Terror*.

67. 'Abdalmalik al-Barrāk, *Rudūd 'alā abāṭīl wa-shubuhāt ḥawl al-jihād* (Amman: al-Nūr, 1997). The book is a polemic against a book on jihad by the comparatively moderate Syrian religious scholar Muḥammad Sa'īd Ramaḍān al-Būṭī.

68. On the topic of jihad, cf. Rudolph Peters, *Jihad in Classical and Modern Islam: A Reader* (Princeton, NJ: Markus Wiener 1996); *idem*, *Islam and Colonialism: The Doctrine of Jihad in Modern History* (The Hague: Mouton, 1979); Cook, *Understanding Jihad.*

69. Ḥāfiẓ al-Karmī, *al-Ṭuyūr al-khuḍr* (Amman: Dār al-Furqān, 1992). On the Islamic concept of martyrdom, cf. Arent Jan Wensinck, 'The Oriental Doctrine of the Martyrs', *Mededeelingen der Koninklijke Akademie van Wetenschappen*, Afdeeling Letterkunde, Deel 53, Serie A no. 6 (1921), pp. 147-74; Etan Kohlberg, 'Medieval Muslim Views of Martyrdom', *Koninklijke Nederlandse Akademie van Wetenschappen, Mededelingen van de Afdeling Letterkunde Nieuwe Reeks*, Deel 60, no. 7 (1997), pp. 281-307; Tilman Seidensticker, 'Martyrdom in Islam', *Awrāq. Estudios sobre el mundo árabe e islámico contemporáneo* 19 (1998), pp. 63-77; Bernard K. Freamon, 'Martyrdom, Suicide, and the Islamic Law of War: A Short Legal History', *Fordham International Law Journal* 27.1 (2003), pp. 299-369 (317-34, 309 n. 25).

70. But cf. Manfred Ullmann, 'Wollte Mohammed Selbstmord begehen?', *Die Welt des Orients* 34 (2004), pp. 64-71 (66).

71. Cf. Franz Rosenthal, 'On Suicide in Islam', *Journal of the American Oriental Society* 66 (1946), pp. 239-59; *idem*, 'Intiḥār', in *The Encyclopaedia of Islam* (Leiden: Brill, new edn, 1960ff.), III, pp. 1246-48; Birgit Krawietz, *Die Ḥurma* (Berlin: Duncker & Humblot, 1991), pp. 91-104; Roberto Denaro, 'Il suicido nell' Islam medievale: un' ipotesi di letteratura della sunna', *Rivista degli Studi Orientali* 70.1-2 (1996), pp. 23-44.

72. Wensinck, 'Doctrine', p. 7.

73. A collection of statements on the problem can be found in Nawāf Hāyil (al-)Takrūrī, *al-'Amaliyyāt al-istishhādiyya fī al-mīzān al-fiqhī* (Damascus: Dār al-Fikr, 4th edn, 2003).

74. Cf. Cook, *Understanding Jihad*, Appendix 3 (pp. 175-81).

75. On the topic of killing civilians, cf. also Thomas Scheffler's contribution to this volume, pp. 37-46 (41).

76. Joseph Croitoru, *Der Märtyrer als Waffe. Die historischen Wurzeln des Selbstmordattentats* (Munich: Hanser, 2003).

77. Cf. Freamon, 'Martyrdom', pp. 334-48.

78. Farhad Khosrokhavar, *L'islamisme et la mort. Le martyre révolutionnaire en Iran* (Paris: L'Harmattan, 1995), pp. 171-221.

79. Christoph Reuter, *My Life is a Weapon: A Modern History of Suicide Bombing* (Princeton, NJ: Princeton University Press, 2004), Chapter 3.

80. Luca Ricolfi, 'Palestinians, 1981–2003', in Diego Gambetta (ed.), *Making Sense of Suicide Missions* (Oxford: Oxford University Press, 2005), pp. 80, 86-87.

81. Ami Pedahzur, *Suicide Terrorism* (Cambridge: Polity Press, 2005), p. 241. Others, among them the Syrians, are also made responsible.

82. For a selection of their verses in English translation, cf. Seidensticker, 'Martyrdom', pp. 66-67.

83. All three waves are treated very informatively in Stephen Frederic Dale, 'Religious Suicide in Islamic Asia: Anticolonial Terrorism in India, Indonesia, and the Philippines', *Journal of Conflict Resolution* 31.1 (1988), pp. 37-59. On the Malabar coast, cf. also *idem*, 'The Islamic Frontier in Southwest India: The shahīd

as a Cultural Ideal Among the Mappillas of Malabar', *Modern Asia Studies* 11.1 (1977), pp. 41-55. For the southern Philippines, cf. also J. Franklin Ewing, 'Juramentado: Institutionalized Suicide among the Moros of the Philippines', *Anthropological Quarterly* 28.4 (1955), pp. 148-55; Cesar Adib Majul, *Muslims in the Philippines* (Quezon: University of the Philippines Press, 1973), especially Chapter 8 ('The Decline of the Sultanates') and Appendix B, 'The Institution of the Juramentado'; Vic Hurley, *Swish of the Kris: The Story of the Moros* (New York: Dutton, 1936) (the book is very rare in European libraries but is available online: http://bakbakan.com under 'Historical features' [accessed 22 August 2006]).

84. Croitoru, *Märtyrer*, pp. 209-13; Stephen Hopgood, 'Tamil Tigers, 1987–2002', in Gambetta (ed.), *Making Sense of Suicide Missions*, pp. 43-76.

85. Croitoru, *Märtyrer*, Chapter 1 ('Das Reich des Tenno im Griff der Militärs'); Peter Hill, 'Kamikaze, 1943–5', in Gambetta (ed.), *Making Sense of Suicide Missions*, pp. 1-41.

86. Stathis Kalyvas and Ignacio Sánchez-Cuenca, 'Killing without Dying: The Absence of Suicide Missions', in Gambetta (ed.), *Making Sense of Suicide Missions*, pp. 209-32 (232).

87. Pedahzur, *Suicide Terrorism*, p. 195.

88. G.W. Bush, 'Address to a Joint Session of Congress and the American People', 20 September 2001, online: http://www.whitehouse.gov/news/releases/2001/09/20010920-8.html (accessed 22 August 2006). Repr. in George W. Bush, *'We will Prevail': President George W. Bush on War, Terrorism, and Freedom* (selected and ed. National Review; New York: Continuum, 2003), p. 14.

89. G.W. Bush, 'President Rallies Troops at Travis Air Force Base', 17 October 2001, online: http://www.whitehouse.gov/news/releases/2001/10/20011017-20.html (accessed 22 August 2006), and *idem*, *'We will Prevail'*, p. 46.

90. Cf. Robert A. Pape, *Dying to Win: The Strategic Logic of Suicide Terrorism* (New York: Random House, 2005), pp. 20-24.

91. Cf. Brian Whitaker, 'Chilling Document hints at Armageddon', *Guardian*, 1 October 2001, online: http://www.guardian.co.uk/Archive/Article/0,4273,4267875,00.html (accessed 22 August 2006).

92. Thomas Scheffler, 'Apocalypticism, Innerwordly Eschatology, and Islamic Extremism', in I. Bellér-Hann and Lisette Gebhardt (eds.), *Religion und Gewalt: Japan, der Nahe Osten und Südasien* (Halle: Orientwissenschaftliches Zentrum der Martin-Luther-Universität Halle-Wittenberg, 2003), pp. 43-79.

93. Steve Coll, *Ghost Wars: The Secret History of the CIA, Afghanistan and Bin Laden, from the Soviet Invasion to September 10, 2001* (New York: Penguin, 2003), p. 319.

94. Coll, *Ghost Wars*, p. 411. On the 1998 attacks, see also Paul R. Pillar, *Terrorism and U.S. Foreign Policy* (Washington, DC: Brookings Institution, 2001), pp. 100, 102-107; Daniel Benjamin and Steven Simon, *The Age of Sacred Terror: Radical Islam's War Against America* (New York: Random House, 2003), pp. 259-61, 352-63, 368-70.

95. Bin Ladin = Usāma Ibn Muḥammad Ibn Lādin, 'I'lān al-jihād 'alā al-amrīkiyyīn al-muḥtallīn li-bilād al-ḥaramayn', *al-Quds al-'Arabī* (23 August 1996), p. 1.

96. 'Naṣṣ bayān al-jabha al-islāmiyya al-'ālamiyya li-jihād al-yahūd wa-l-ṣalībiyyīn', *al-Quds al-'Arabī* (23 February 1998), p. 3.

97. For a documentation of Bin Ladin's pre-9/11 interviews see Thomas Hegghammer (ed.), *Dokumentasjon om al-Qaida—Intervjuer, kommunikéer og andre primærkilder, 1990–2002* (Kjeller, Norway: Forsvarets Forskningsinstitutt, 2003), pp. 15-88; online: http://rapporter.ffi.no/rapporter/2002/01393.pdf [accessed 22 August 2006]).

98. On the symbiotic relationship between al-Qaeda statements and the rise of al-Jazeera TV, see Hugh Miles, *Al-Jazeera: How Arab TV News Challenged the World* (London: Abacus, 2005), pp. 107-219.

99. Abdel Bari Atwan, *The Secret History of al-Qa'ida* (London: Saqi, 2006), pp. 120-49; Brynjar Lia, 'Al-Qaeda Online: Understanding Jihadist Internet Infrastructure', *Jane's Intelligence Review*, 1 January 2006, online: http://www.mil.no/multimedia/archive/00075/Al-Qaeda_online__und_75416a.pdf (accessed 22 August 2006).

100. The most comprehensive semi-public collections of al-Qaeda-related documents between 1990 and 2004 in English translation are Hegghammer, *Dokumentasjon*; and *idem*, *Al-Qaida Statements 2003–2004* (Kjeller, Norway: Forsvarets Forskningsinstitutt 2005; online: http://rapporter.ffi.no/rapporter/2005/01428.pdf [accessed 22 August 2006]). Good selections have been published in Lawrence (ed.), *Messages to the World*; Gilles Kepel and Jean-Pierre Milelli (eds.), *Al-Qaida dans le texte* (Paris: Presses Universitaires de France, 2005); Randall B. Hamud (ed.), *Osama bin Laden: America's Enemy in His Own Words* (San Diego, CA: Nadeem, 2005); Marwan Abou-Taam and Ruth Bigalke (eds.), *Die Reden des Osama bin Laden* (Munich: Diederichs, 2006).

101. Peter L. Bergen, *Holy War, Inc.: Inside the Secret World of Osama bin Laden* (London: Phoenix, 2002), p. 226.

102. World Islamic Front, 'Naṣṣ bayān' (English translation in Lawrence, *Messages*, p. 60).

103. Bin Ladin, Statement on al-Jazeera TV, 3 November 2001 (English translation in Lawrence, *Messages*, p. 136).

104. World Islamic Front, 'Naṣṣ bayān' (English translation in Lawrence, *Messages*, 61).

105. Abū Ghayth, Statement on al-Jazeera TV, 13 October 2001 (English translation in Hegghammer, *Dokumentasjon*, p. 155).

106. Bin Ladin, 'I'lān al-jihād' (English translation in Yonah Alexander and Michael S. Swetnam, *Usama bin Laden's al-Qaida* [Ardsley, NY: Transnational Publishers, 2001], Appendix 1 A, pp. 8-9).

107. Bin Ladin, 'I'lān al-jihād' (English translation in Alexander and Swetnam, *al-Qaida*, 1 A, p. 11).

108. World Islamic Front, 'Naṣṣ bayān' (English translation in Lawrence, *Messages*, p. 61).

109. Cf. Atwan, *Secret History*, pp. 78-79.

110. Bin Ladin, Interview with Ḥāmid Mīr, 7 November 2001 (English translation in Lawrence, *Messages*, pp. 140, 141).

111. Bin Ladin, Interviews with John Miller, 28 May 1998 (English translation in Hegghammer, *Dokumentasjon*, pp. 44-45), Taysīr 'Allūnī, 21 October 2001 (English translation in Lawrence, *Messages*, pp. 117-19, 126); Ḥāmid Mīr (English translation in Lawrence, *Messages*, p. 140).

112. Bin Ladin, Interviews with John Miller (English translation in Hegghammer, *Dokumentasjon*, p. 44) and Taysīr 'Allūnī (Lawrence, *Messages*, pp. 114, 119).

113. Bin Ladin, Interview with Ḥāmid Mīr (English translation in Lawrence, *Messages*, p. 140).

114. Bin Ladin, Interviews with John Miller (English translation in Hegghammer, *Dokumentasjon*, p. 42) and Ḥāmid Mīr (Lawrence, *Messages*, pp. 140-41).

115. Ayman al-Ẓawāhirī, *Fursān taḥta rāyat al-nabī* [Knights under the Prophet's Banner], in *al-Sharq al-Awsaṭ*, 2–12 December 2001, pt. 11.

116. Bin Ladin, Statement on al-Jazeera TV, 7 October 2001 (English translation in Lawrence, *Messages*, p. 105); see also his interview with Ḥāmid Mīr (English translation in Lawrence, *Messages*, p. 141).

117. Bin Ladin, 'I'lān al-jihād' (English translation in Alexander and Swetnam, *al-Qaida*, 1 A, p. 7).

118. Bin Ladin, 'I'lān al-jihād' (English translation in Alexander and Swetnam, *al-Qaida*, 1 A, pp. 11-12).

119. Bin Ladin, Interview with Taysīr 'Allūnī (English translation in Lawrence, *Messages*, 111-12).

120. Bin Ladin, Statement on al-Jazeera TV, 26 December 2001 (English translation in Lawrence, *Messages*, p. 151).

121. Bin Ladin, 'I'lān al-jihād' (English translation in Alexander and Swetnam, *al-Qaida*, 1 A, p. 2).

122. Navid Kermani, 'A Dynamite of the Spirit: Why Nietzsche, Not the Koran is the Key to Understanding the Suicide Bombers', *The Times Literary Supplement* (29 March 2002), p. 15; Olivier Roy, *Globalised Islam: The Search for a New Ummah* (London: Hurst, 2005), p. 294 (cf. also pp. 324-25).

123. Benjamin and Simon, *Sacred Terror*, pp. 71, 91-93, 418, 424-46; Richard Landes, 'Apocalyptic Islam and Bin Laden' [n.d.], online: http://www.bu.edu/mille/people/rlpages/Bin_Laden.html (accessed 22 August 2006); Cook, *Understanding Jihad*, pp. 157-61.

124. See, e.g., Paul Berman, *Terror and Liberalism* (New York: W.W. Norton, 2003), pp. 52-102; Frederick W. Kagan, *The New Bolcheviks: Understanding Al Qaeda* (Washington, DC: American Enterprise Institute, 2005) (*National Security Outlook*, November 2005).

125. Pape, *Dying to Win*; François Burgat, *L'islamisme à l'heure d'Al-Qaida* (Paris: La Découverte, 2005).

126. Cf. Peter L. Bergen, *The Osama bin Laden I Know: An Oral History of al Qaeda's Leader* (New York: Free Press, 2005), pp. 2, 8.

127. Robert Fisk, 'Anti-Soviet Warrior Puts his Army on the Road to Peace', *The Independent* (6 December 1993). See also Atwan, *Secret History*, p. 77. On the Koranic concept of *sakīna* see Koran 2:248; 9:26, 40; 48:4, 18, 26.

128. See, for example, CNN's transcript of a discussion of Bin Ladin with Arab visitors, video-taped in mid-November 2001, online: http://www.cnn.com/2001/US/12/13/tape.transcript (accessed 22 August 2006); Atwan, *Secret History*, p. 111; Robert Fisk, *The Great War for Civilization* (New York: Knopf, 2005), pp. 19, 29-30; Coll, *Ghost Wars*, pp. 288-89.

129. *Sunna* refers to the sayings and actions of the Prophet Muḥammad, the reports of which *(ḥadīth*, pl. *aḥādīth)* were compiled in large collections. Next to the Koran, the Sunna is the second pillar of Islamic divine law.

130. Atwan, *Secret History*, p. 31.

131. *Al-Mahdī* (Arabic: 'The rightly guided one'): messianic figure expected to appear in the End Times to restore justice on earth; *al-Dajjāl* (Arabic: 'the deceiver'): Islamic equivalent to the Anti-Christ; *Ya'jūj wa-Ma'jūj* (Gog and Magog): two mythological peoples, presumably from Central Asian or Turkish origin, expected to appear in the End Times after the Dajjāl in order to be killed by God in response to a prayer of *'Īsā Ibn Maryam* (Jesus), who will establish the exclusive rule of the *sharī'a* and abolish the *jizya* (the poll-tax for non-Muslims under Islamic law), that is, close the legal loopholes that allow Christians and Jews to remain non-Muslims under the roof of Muslim law before the End Times. After the final descent of Jesus, nothing but conversion to Islam will be accepted from non-Muslims.

132. See, for instance, *Ṣaḥīḥ al-Bukhārī*, IV, book 52, nos. 176, 177; referred to by Bin Ladin in his interviews with John Miller (English translation in Hegghammer, *Dokumentasjon*, p. 46) and Taysīr 'Allūnī (Lawrence, *Messages*, p. 125).

133. Cf. Bin Ladin, Interview with Taysīr 'Allūnī (English translation in Lawrence, *Messages*, p. 109). See also his interview with John Miller (English translation in Hegghammer, *Dokumentasjon*, p. 46).

134. Bin Ladin, Interview with John Miller (English translation in Hegghammer, *Dokumentasjon*, p. 47).

135. Bin Laden, Statement on al-Jazeera TV, 26 December 2001 (English translation in Lawrence, *Messages*, p. 149). *Hubal* was the most popular pagan deity in pre-Islamic Mecca. His statue in the Ka'ba was destroyed when the Prophet captured Mecca in 630.

136. Ernst-Dieter Hehl, 'Was ist eigentlich ein Kreuzzug?' *Historische Zeitschrift* 259 (1994), pp. 303-305, 316, 328, 334.

137. See, e.g., Bruce Lincoln, *Holy Terrors: Thinking about Religion after September 11* (Chicago: University of Chicago Press, 2003), pp. 13-15, 60; *The 9/11 Commission Report*, p. 51; Fawaz A. Gerges, *The Far Enemy: Why Jihad Went Global* (New York: Cambridge University Press, 2005), pp. 4-9; Kagan, 'New Bolcheviks'; Atwan, *Secret History*, pp. 72-73.

138. Karen Armstrong, 'The Label of Catholic Terror Was Never Used for the IRA', *Guardian* (11 July 2005).

139. Sayyid Quṭb, *Ma'ālim fī al-ṭarīq* [1964] (Cairo: Dār al-Shurūq, 13th edn, 1989), Chapter 4, pp. 62-91 (English translation: Quṭb, *Milestones* [Delhi: Markazi Maktaba Islami, 3rd edn, 1991], pp. 93-140).

140. That began to change in 2001 when, to Bin Ladin's disappointment, most Muslims failed to rise against the American invasion of Afghanistan. Cf. his interview with Taysīr 'Allūnī (English translation in Lawrence, *Messages*, pp. 120-24).

141. William E. Shepard, 'Islam as a "System" in the Later Writings of Sayyid Qutb', *Middle Eastern Studies* 25.1 (1989), pp. 31-50.

142. Berman, *Terror*, 52-102; Kagan, 'New Bolcheviks'.

143. Cf. Daniel L. Byman, 'Al-Qaeda as an Adversary: Do We Understand Our Enemy?', *World Politics* 56 (2003), pp. 153-56.

144. Bergen, *The Osama bin Laden I Know*, pp. 364-65.

145. Mark Sedgwick, 'Al-Qaeda and the Nature of Religious Terrorism', *Terrorism and Political Violence* 16.4 (2004), pp. 801-804. The 'Propaganda of the Deed' was a strategic concept that first emerged among European Anarchists in the second half of the nineteenth century. Its proponents assumed that direct action, for example, the spectacular assassination of an oppressive ruler, would do more to mobilize and educate the 'masses' than thousands of speeches, articles, and books.

146. Gerges, *Far Enemy*, pp. 99-118.

147. Steven Emerson and Khalid Duran, 'Interview with Abu Iman', 4 November 1993, quoted in Evan F. Kohlmann, *Al-Qaida's Jihad in Europe* (Oxford: Berg, 2004), p. 6.

148. The two declarations of war quote, among others, the Mālikī jurist al-Qurṭubī (d. 1172), the Ḥanafī jurist al-Kāsānī (d. 1189), the Ḥanbalī scholars Ibn Qudāma (d. 1223), Ibn Taymiyya (d. 1328), and Ibn Qayyim al-Jawziyya (d. 1350), and Shāfi'ī scholars like Ibn Kathīr (d. 1373) or al-Shawkānī (d. 1834).

149. See Rohan Gunaratna, *Inside Al Qaeda: Global Network of Terror* (New York: Berkley Books, 2003), pp. 166-67.

150. Experts assume that the term 'al-Qaeda', being the name of a distinct Islamist organization, has lost much of its political relevance since 2001 and prefer to speak instead of 'global Jihadism' as a worldwide phenomenon of ideologically, but not hierarchically interrelated local networks that draw part of their inspiration from the deeds and speeches of Bin Ladin and his companions. See Thomas Hegghammer, 'Global Jihadism after the Iraq War', *Middle East Journal* 60.1 (2006), pp. 11-32.

151. Max Weber, 'Some Categories of Interpretive Sociology' (in German, 1913; trans. E.E. Graber), *The Sociological Quarterly* 22 (1981), pp. 151-80 (quotation p. 152).

152. Diego Gambetta, 'Can We Make Sense of Suicide Missions?', in *idem* (ed.), *Making Sense of Suicide Missions*, pp. 259-99.

153. McDermott, *Perfect Soldiers*, quotations pp. xvi and xvii.

154. Stephen Holmes, 'Al-Qaeda, September 11, 2001', in Gambetta (ed.), *Making Sense of Suicide Missions*, pp. 131-72; see p. 140 on Mohamed Atta's anger towards Egypt and its Westernized culture.

155. Fouda and Fielding, *Masterminds of Terror*, pp. 108, 121 n. 10.

156. Cook, *Understanding Jihad*, quotation p. 6.

157. Albrecht Noth, *Heiliger Krieg und Heiliger Kampf im Islam und Christentum: Beiträge zur Vorgeschichte und Geschichte der Kreuzzüge* (Bonn: Röhrscheid, 1966), pp. 52-53. The entry 'rahbānīya', in *Shorter Encyclopedia of Islam* (Leiden: Brill, 1974), pp. 466-67, gives the sources for the alleged saying.

158. Noth, *Heiliger Krieg und Heiliger Kampf*, pp. 55-56 (translation HGK).

159. Noth, *Heiliger Krieg und Heiliger Kampf*, p. 61 (translation HGK).

160. Hartmut Esser, *Soziologie. Spezielle Grundlagen. Band 1: Situationslogik und Handeln* (Frankfurt: Campus, 1999), p. 63. Chapter 2 deals with the 'Thomas-Theorem', Chapter 5 with the definition of the situation; see *idem*, 'Die Definition der Situation', *Kölner Zeitschrift für Soziologie und Sozialpsychologie* 48 (1996), pp. 1-34. Cf. Robert K. Merton, 'The Thomas Theorem and the Matthew Effect', *Social Forces* 74 (1995), pp. 379-424.

161. Hans Joas, *The Creativity of Action* (Chicago: University of Chicago Press, 1997), pp. 148-67, especially p. 160.

162. The naval metaphor of a sextant is used by Gerd Baumann to express the same idea; see *The Multicultural Riddle: Rethinking National, Ethnic, and Religious Identities* (London: Routledge, 1999), p. 69.

163. Joseph Schacht, *An Introduction to Islamic Law* (Oxford: Clarendon Press, 1964), p. 116.

164. Guido Steinberg, *Der nahe und der ferne Feind. Die Netzwerke des islamistischen Terrorismus* (Munich: C.H. Beck, 2005), p. 41. For the doctrine of Muhammad Quṭb compared with his brother's, cf. Sabine Damir-Geilsdorf, *Herrschaft und Gesellschaft. Der islamische Wegbereiter Sayyid Quṭb und seine Rezeption* (Würzburg: Ergon, 2003), pp. 294-99.

165. David Cook, 'Suicide Attacks or "Martyrdom Operations" in Contemporary *Jihad* Literature', *Nova Religio* 6 (2002), pp. 7-44 (here pp. 19-21).

166. We know from Fouda's interview with Binalshib that the Capitol and not the White House was the target of the plane that crashed prematurely in Pennsylvania (Fouda and Fielding, *Masterminds of Terror*, pp. 127-28).

167. Johannes J.G. Jansen, *The Neglected Duty: The Creed of Sadat's Assassins and Islamic Resurgence in the Middle East* (New York: Macmillan, 1986), §84-90, pp. 199-201.

168. Roland Jacquard, *In the Name of Osama Bin Laden: Global Terrorism and the Bin Laden Brotherhood* (Durham: Duke University Press, 2002 [French edn 2001]), p. 60 and Appendix document 12, pp. 200-201.

169. The excerpt of the alleged fifth page of the document in the Washington Post refers likewise to that concept. The attackers should remember the battle of the Prophet against the infidels when he set out to build the Islamic state.

170. W. Montgomery Watt, *Muhammad: Prophet and Statesman* (Oxford: Oxford University Press, 1961), pp. 102-26.

171. For the main studies on the issue, see Wael B. Hallaq, *A History of Islamic Legal Theories: An Introduction to Sunni 'usul al-fiqh'* (Cambridge: Cambridge University Press, 1997), pp. 68-74 (deals with the different opinions of jurists regarding abrogation); Yasin Dutton, *The Origins of Islamic Law* (London: RoutledgeCurzon, 1999), pp. 121-25 (introduces past and contemporary debates on the principle); John Burton, 'The Exegesis of Q. 2:106 and the Islamic Theories of Naskh', *Bulletin of the School of Oriental and African Studies* 48 (1985), pp. 452-69; Ruthven (*A Fury for God*, pp. 42, 47-52) points to scholars who interpret Koran 2:106 as referring to revelations to Jews and Christians, not to Muḥammad.

172. Jansen, *The Neglected Duty*, §76-79, pp. 195-96.

173. Abdullahi Ahmed An-Na'im, *Toward an Islamic Reformation: Civil Liberties, Human Rights, and International Law* (Syracuse, NY: Syracuse University Press, 1990), pp. 52-60, relies on the authority of the Sudanese scholar Mahmud Muhammad Taha, who discerned two stages of the message of Islam: one represented by the period of Mecca, the other by the subsequent Medina period. Taha maintained that the earlier message was in fact the eternal and fundamental one; it emphasized the inherent dignity of all human beings, regardless of gender, religious belief, race, and so on. Only after that message was violently rejected by the people of Mecca was the more realistic message of Medina implemented. The suspended

aspects of the Mecca message were not abrogated in principle, but only postponed for implementation under appropriate circumstances in the future. Under the present circumstances, the development of Islamic law should return from the Medina stage back to the Mecca stage. By placing Muḥammad's revelations in their historical settings, Taha and An-Na'im envision an Islamic order that incorporates women and non-Muslims on equal terms. The approach is similar to what happened in modern Jewish and Christian theology, when historians dissected the Bible in different sources each with a validity of their own.

174. Cole, in his examination of the psychology of the document, noted remarkable agreements with Sufis and Muslim Brothers: 'Al-Qaeda's Doomsday Document and Psychological Manipulation'. He translates the word *tanbīh* as 'admonition', in the sense of an admonition of the 'base self' *(al-nafs)*.

175. Khaled Abou El Fadl, '9/11 and the Muslim Transformation', in Mary L. Dudziak (ed.), *September 11 in History: A Watershed Moment?* (Durham: Duke University Press, 2003), pp. 70-111 (here pp. 81-86).

176. Cook, *Understanding Jihad*, pp. 136-39 ('The Conspiracy to Destroy Islam'); *idem*, *Contemporary Muslim Apocalyptic Literature* (Syracuse, NY: Syracuse University Press, 2005), pp. 180-83 ('The Final Battle').

177. Etan Kohlberg, 'Taqiyya in Shi'i Theology and Religion', in Hans G. Kippenberg and Guy G. Stroumsa (eds.), *Secrecy and Concealment: Studies in the History of Mediterranean and Near Eastern Religions* (Leiden: Brill, 1995), pp. 345-80.

178. See, for example, Ruthven, *A Fury for God*, p. 300.

179. There is a tension between martyrdom as one's own deed and martyrdom as bestowed by God; cf. Ivan Strenski, 'Sacrifice, Gift and the Social Logic of Muslim "Human Bombers"', *Terrorism and Political Violence* 15 (2003), pp. 1-34 (here pp. 12-13); Mneimneh and Makiya, 'Manual for a "Raid"', p. 317.

180. Ruthven, *A Fury for God*, p. 102.

181. Cook, 'Suicide Attacks or "Martyrdom Operations" ', p. 23

182. Cook, 'Suicide Attacks or "Martyrdom Operations"', p. 27.

183. Martin Kramer, *Hezbollah's Vision of the West* (Washington: Institute for Near East Policy, 1989), Policy Papers, 16, pp. 37-39 (quotation p. 38).

184. '11 September, Terrorism, Islam, and the Intifada' (Interview with Shaikh Muhammad Husain Fadlallah), *Journal of Palestine Studies* 31 (2002), pp. 78-84 (here p. 83).

185. Thomas Scheffler, '"Allahu Akbar": Zur Theologie des Widerstandsgeistes im Islam', in André Stanisavljević and Ralf Zwengel (ed.), *Religion und Gewalt: Der Islam nach dem 11. September* (Potsdam: Mostar Friedensprojekt e.V., 2002), pp. 21-46.

186. Scheffler '"Allahu Akbar"', pp. 31-32; the unabridged document in an English translation is published by Yonah Alexander and Michael S. Swetnam, *Usama bin Ladin's al-Qaida: Profile of a Terrorist Network* (New Delhi: Aditya Books, 2001), Appendix 1 A. On Bin Ladin's first declaration of war and its context, see Bergen, *Holy War, Inc.*, Chapter 5.

187. Sayyid Qutb, *Milestones* (Delhi: Aakif, 1985), pp. 29-30; Sabine Damir-Geilsdorf, *Herrschaft und Gesellschaft*, pp. 181-90 ('Jihād-Konzept').

188. Raphael Israeli, 'A Manual of Islamic Fundamentalist Terrorism', *Terrorism and Political Violence* 14 (2002), pp. 23-40 (here p. 35).

189. Roy P. Mottahedeh, *Loyalty and Leadership in an Early Islamic Society* (Princeton, NJ: Princeton University Press, 1980), pp. 50-54.

190. Franz Taeschner, *Zünfte und Bruderschaften im Islam: Texte zur Geschichte der Futuwwa* (Zürich: Artemis, 1979), pp. 97, 159.

191. Richard P. Mitchell, *The Society of the Muslim Brothers* (Oxford: Oxford University Press, 1969, p. 196. According to Juan Cole 'the Muslim Brotherhood tradition in Egypt had not, unlike the Salafis, entirely rejected Sufi ideas' ('Al-Qaeda's Doomsday Document and Psychological Manipulation', online: http://www.juancole.com/essays/qaeda.htm [accessed 22 August 2006]).

192. Jansen, *The Neglected Duty*, pp. 24, 204; Mitchell, *The Society of the Muslim Brothers*, p. 196.

193. McDermott, *Perfect Soldiers*, pp. 63-76 (for a discussion of the apartment in Hamburg-Harburg).

194. McDermott, *Perfect Soldiers*, p. 85.

195. *The 9/11 Commission Report*—compare p. 438 with p. 164.

196. *The 9/11 Commission Report*, pp. 165-66.

197. On Ayman al-Ẓawāhirī, see Esposito, *Unholy War*, pp. 18-20, and Bergen, *The Osama bin Laden I Know*, pp. 63-67.

198. For evidence with regard to the merger, see *The 9/11 Commission Report*, p. 67 with n. 82; Bergen, *The Osama bin Laden I Know*, p. 194; Steinberg, *Der nahe und der ferne Feind*, p. 77.

199. Steinberg, *Der nahe und der ferne Feind*, pp. 59-64.

200. Translation by Yonah Alexander and Michael S. Swetnam (eds.), *Usama bin Laden's ,al-Qaida': Profile of a Terrorist Network* (New Delhi: Aditya Books, 2001), Appendix 1 A, pp. 1-20; abridged translation with annotations by Lawrence (ed.), *Messages to the World*, pp. 23-30 (Statement 3).

201. English Translations by Alexander and Swetnam (eds.), *Usama bin Laden's ,al-Qaida'*, Appendix 1; Lawrence (ed.), *Messages to the World*, pp. 58-62 (Statement 6).

202. Cook, *Understanding Jihad*, pp. 136-39 ('The Conspiracy to Destroy Islam'); *idem*, *Contemporary Muslim Apocalyptic Literature*, pp. 180-83 ('The Final Battle').

203. Alexander and Swetnam (eds.), *Usama bin Laden's ,al-Qaida'*, Appendix 2, p. 2; Lawrence (ed.), *Messages to the World*, p. 61.

204. Translation in Lawrence (ed.), *Messages to the World*, pp. 58-62 (Statement 6); Alexander and Swetnam provide a slightly different translation from Lawrence, 'Ye cling so heavily to the earth?' (*Usama bin Laden's 'al-Qaida'*, Appendix 1 B, p. 3).

205. The distinction between both types of martyrdom has been established by Farhad Khosrokhavar, *Suicide Bombers: Allah's New Martyrs* (London: Pluto 2005 [French edn 2002]). Though the study is mainly on Shi'i subjects, it addresses a similar distinction in Sunni Islam.

206. Jason Burke, *Al-Qaeda: Casting a Shadow of Terror* (London: Tauris, 2003), pp. 7-12.

207. Lawrence (ed.), *Messages to the World*, e.g. p. 108 (see index *s.v.* al-Qaeda).

208. Steinberg, *Der nahe und der ferne Feind*, pp. 59-60.

209. Jacquard, *In the Name of Osama Bin Laden.*

210. Gunaratna, *Inside al Qaeda*, p. 129: 'Within the organization itself, the notion of brotherhood ingrained in Islam helps Al Qaeda cohere'.

211. Burke, *Al-Qaeda: Casting a Shadow of Terror*, pp. 11-12.

212. Cf. Burke, *Al-Qaeda: Casting a Shadow of Terror*, pp. 13-22.

213. For a reconstruction of the (three) stages of joining al-Qaeda, see Marc Sageman, *Understanding Terror Networks* (Philadelphia: University of Pennsylvania Press, 2004), pp. 99-135; on pp. 120-21 he deals with 'Formal Acceptance'.

214. Bergen, *The Osama bin Laden I Know*, pp. 74-107 ('The Birth of al Qaeda'), oath p. 81.

215. Bergen, *The Osama bin Laden I Know*, p. 86; for further examples, see pp. 102, 117, 138-39, 263.

216. Sageman, *Understanding Terror Networks*, p. 121.

217. Sageman, *Understanding Terror Networks*, pp. 107-20 ('social affiliation').

218. Sageman, *Understanding Terror Networks*, quotations pp. 122 and 123.

219. Jacquard, *In the Name of Osama Bin Laden*, pp. 55-72 ('The Islamic Legion').

220. Renate Mayntz, 'Hierarchie oder Netzwerk? Zu den Organisationsformen des Terrorismus', *Berliner Journal für Soziologie* 14 (2004), pp. 251-62.

221. Sageman, *Understanding Terror Networks*, p. 121, referring to Mark Granovetter, 'The Strength of Weak Ties', *American Journal of Sociology* 78 (1973), pp. 1360-80. Cf. Jens Beckert, 'Soziologische Netzwerkanalyse', in Dirk Kaesler (ed.), *Aktuelle Theorien der Soziologie. Von Shmuel N. Eisenstadt bis zur Postmoderne* (Munich: C.H. Beck, 2005), pp. 286-312 (here 289-93).

222. John R. Hall, 'Apocalypse 9/11', in Phillip Charles Lucas and Thomas Robbins (eds.), *New Religious Movements in the Twenty-First Century: Legal, Political, and Social Challenges in Global Perspective* (Routledge: London, 2004), pp. 265-82 (here p. 273).

223. Ruthven, *A Fury for God*, pp. 51-53; on Ibn Khaldun's model for the rise of urban dynasties in North Africa see Ernest Gellner, *Muslim Society* (Cambridge: Cambridge University Press, 1981), pp. 1-85.

224. Burke, *Al-Qaeda: Casting a Shadow of Terror*, pp. 15 and 16.

225. Georg Elwert, 'Charismatische Mobilisierung und Gewaltmärkte. Die Attentäter des 11. September', in Wolfgang Bergsdorf, Dietmar Herz, and Hans Hoffmeister (eds.), *Gewalt und Terror. 11 Vorlesungen* (Weimar: Rhino, 2003), pp. 91-117.

226. *The 9/11 Commission Report*, pp. 169-73; Gunaratna, *Inside al Qaeda*, S. 80-92 ('Financial Network'), and Jacquard, *In the Name of Osama Bin Laden*, Chapter 11 ('The Bin Laden's Network's Billions').

227. *The 9/11 Commission Report*, pp. 155-60; Burke, *al-Qaeda: Casting a Shadow of Terror*, pp. 220-21.

228. *The 9/11 Commission Report*, pp. 160-65; McDermott, *Perfect Soldiers*, pp. 179-80.

229. For more details, see *The 9/11 Commission Report*, p. 166; McDermott, *Perfect Soldiers*, pp. 179-80.

230. *The 9/11 Commission Report*, p. 225.

231. *The 9/11 Commission Report*, p. 223.

232. *The 9/11 Commission Report*, p. 231; Burke, *Al-Qaeda: Casting a Shadow of Terror*, p. 213.

233. Quoted by Mneimneh and Makiya, 'Manual for a "Raid"', pp. 303-304 n. 2.

234. Gerhard Endress, *Einführung in die islamische Geschichte* (Munich: C.H. Beck, 1982), p. 177.

235. Fouda and Fielding, *Masterminds of Terror*, pp. 110-13.

236. Concerning the notion of the 'living martyr', who confessed an attack before committing it, see Pedahzur, *Suicide Terrorism*, p. 179.

237. Stephan Rosiny, *Islamismus bei den Schiiten im Libanon: Religion im Übergang von Tradition zur Moderne* (Berlin: Das arabische Buch, 1996), pp. 123-36.

238. Peter Waldmann, *Terrorismus: Provokation der Macht* (Munich: Gerling Akademie, 1998), pp. 61-68.

239. Magnus Ranstorp, *Hizb'allah in Lebanon: The Politics of the Western Hostage Crisis* (New York: St. Martin's Press, 1997), pp. 62-65 ('Use of Cover Names and Concealment by Hizb'allah in Abduction of Foreigners').

240. Mitchell, *The Society of the Muslim Brothers*, p. 32 (history); p. 177 (diagram of the organisation); pp. 195-200 (function of the basic units).

241. Denis Engelleder, *Die islamistische Bewegung in Jordanien und Palästina 1945–1989* (Wiesbaden: Harrassowitz, 2002), pp. 108-11; Johannes Reissner, *Ideologie und Politik der Muslimbrüder Syriens: Von den Wahlen 1947 bis zum Verbot unter Adib Ash-Shishakli 1952* (Freiburg: Schwarz, 1980), p. 103.

242. Mitchell, *The Society of the Muslim Brothers*, pp. 195-200; Engelleder, *Die islamistische Bewegung*, pp. 108-11; Emmanuel Sivan, 'The Enclave Culture', in Martin E. Marty and R. Scott Appleby (eds.), *Fundamentalism Comprehended* (Chicago: University of Chicago Press, 1995), pp. 11-63.

243. Gilles Kepel, *Muslim Extremism in Egypt: The Prophet and Pharaoh* (Berkeley: University of California Press, 2003 [French edn 1984]), pp. 52-56.

244. Hans H. Gerth and C. Wright Mills, *From Max Weber: Essays in Sociology* (Oxford: Oxford University Press, 1946), p. 278.

245. Max Weber, *Economy and Society* (ed. Guenther Roth and Claus Wittich; 3 vols.; Berkeley: University of California Press, 1978), I, pp. 544-55.

246. Olivier Roy, *Globalized Islam: The Search for a New Ummah* (New York: Columbia University Press, 2004), p. 97.

247. Roy, *Globalized Islam*, pp. 5-6.

248. Roy, *Globalized Islam*, S.20.

249. McDermott, *Perfect Soldiers*, pp. xvi-xvii.

250. Holmes, 'Al-Qaeda, September 11, 2001'.

251. Excerpts from the video were transmitted by several TV stations. A screenshot is reproduced in *Der Spiegel* 19 (2005), p. 64, bottom.

252. This is an allusion to a Prophetic tradition transmitted in 'Abdallāh Ibn al-Mubārak's *Kitāb al-Jihād* (no. 30): 'Dust [stirred up during a campaign] for the

cause of God and the smoke of hell will never be united in the nostrils of a Muslim servant [of God]' (*lā tajtami'u ghubārun fī sabīli llāhi wa-dukhānu jahannama fī mankhiray 'abdin muslimin abadan*). What is meant is that nobody who participated in jihad will go to hell.

253. These last words are an allusion to Koran surah 2 verse 154: 'And call not those who are slain in the way of God dead. Nay, they are living', and surah 3 verse 169: 'Think not of those who are slain in the way of God as dead. Nay, they are living'.

254. On these two persons, cf. *The Encyclopaedia of Islam* (12 vols.; Leiden: Brill, 1960–2004), III, p. 879; II, p. 936.

255. E.g. at www.islaam.net under the heading 'Knowledge': 'Nashids', and http://www.enshad.net/htm/singers/Tareq_Abu_Zeyad/Ya_3aBed_Al-7aramayn (accessed 22 August 2006).

256. For background on the religious *nashīd*, cf. Michael Frishkopf: 'Islamic Hymnody in Egypt: *al-Inshād al-Dīnī*', in *The Garland Encyclopedia of World Music*, VI (New York: Routledge, 2002), pp. 165-75; Patrick Haenni and Husam Tammam, 'Chat Shows, nashid Groups and Lite Preaching: Egypt's Air-conditioned Islam', *Le Monde diplomatique*, English edn, September 2003, online: http://mondediplo.com/2003/09/03egyptislam (accessed 22 August 2006).

257. Nāṣir al-Dīn al-Albānī was a watch repairman by trade and self-taught authority on Prophetic tradition and Islamic law. Because of his non-conformist views and aggressiveness, he was expelled from Syria and then from Saudi Arabia and spent the last years of his life until his death in 1999 under house arrest in Amman, Jordan.

258. In Arabic: *al-Sharq al-Awsaṭ*; English subtitle: 'Pan-Arab daily published from London'.

259. See online: http://www.asharqalawsat.com/details.asp?section=4&article=194981&issue=9069 (accessed 22 August 2006). In Arabic the title is *Jadal bayn al-uṣūliyyīn ḥawl istikhdām ashriṭat 'al-ḥūr al-'īn' li-tajnīd muqātilīn li-'al-Qā'ida'*.

260. See online: http://balsam99.jeeran.com/B_99.html. A download of the files under *'ushshāq al-ḥūr* is not possible (accessed 22 August 2006).

261. This is, of course, an allusion to the fifth verse of the song of scene 5 presented above.

262. 'Umar al-Bakrī, often spelled Omar Bakri (Mohammed), left Great Britain after the attacks of 7 July 2005, and now lives in Beirut.

263. al-'Aynā' is mentioned in 'Abdallāh Ibn Mubārak's *Kitāb al-Jihād*, no. 149; on her face's extinguishing the sun's light, see no. 24.

264. This edition is based on the Arabic text edited by Albrecht Fuess, Moez Khalfaoui, and Tilman Seidensticker, in Kippenberg and Seidensticker (eds.), *Terror im Dienste Gottes*.

Index of Names

INDEX OF SUBJECTS

CPSIA information can be obtained at www.ICGtesting.com
Printed in the USA
LVOW082022291111

257038LV00002B/2/A

9 781845 531294